From The Case Files of

 and

Claire Welch

Contents

Gangs

Introduction

In the early part of the 20th century there was real concern about the influence that cocaine was having on the population of the United States. Abuse of this substance had had the potential to become a problem during the First World War (1914–18), but had never really taken off in Britain. At a time when cultures were markedly different on both sides of the Atlantic, cocaine fitted perfectly with the extravagance of an affluent American lifestyle – a "champagne" drug – but didn't find a firm footing in the UK until much later, during the 1970s and into the 1980s. Although it was essentially a luxury, cocaine had been a part of everyday life for some cultures for many thousands of years. The components of this drug are found in the cocoa leaf, and archaeologists found remaining matter of these leaves dating back to approximately AD 500 at burial sites in Peru. It was clear that cocoa leaves had been chewed by cocoa-growing communities for more than 15 centuries, and Spain was to become pivotal in this drug's emergence in Europe, not once, but twice.

The Spanish, having conquered the Incas, first brought cocoa leaves to Europe after discovering how robust and invigorated the local populations were after using it. The drug was clearly a stimulant that negated the need for much sleep or food and, as a result, hunger was kept at bay while longer working hours were possible. It wasn't long before the Spanish began paying the Incas in cocoa leaves and, when Phillip II declared the drug "essential" to the workforces of the conquered territories, the leaves made the long journey to Europe where, at first, they were received with little enthusiasm. For the better part of 300 years, the effects of cocoa had little place in the European way of life until German scientist Friedrich Gaedecke identified the active ingredient of the leaf in 1855. It took another four years before Albert Niemann, having managed to isolate the compound, called it cocaine. Despite its addictive nature, cocaine began to weave its way into the fabric of everyday living during the latter part of the 19th century. Many of the famous were to sample its delights, including the adventurer Ernest Shackleton. It made its way into food and drinks, and the advent of chewing gum laced with cocaine, Vin Mariani and Coca Cola – which, up until 1903, contained 60mg of the drug – fuelled the problem further. There was little or no information on the harm that cocaine could do, despite rising numbers of paranoid users who quickly became addicted, and for almost 70 years the virtues of the drug were widely praised by royalty, doctors and religious leaders alike. However, all that was about to change when, in 1916, it became illegal to possess or take cocaine without a prescription. In 1920, the Dangerous Drugs Act was passed. Cocaine was to remain "in hiding" for the best part of 60 years before it reared its ugly head and caused the most devastation it had yet. It became one of the driving forces of many of today's modern gangs, and the warnings about the drug's potential to infiltrate British society came, far too little, too late, in the mid-1980s. The Spanish had already established an infrastructure between South America and Europe, and the contacts were beginning to grow. The damage had already been done and, for the second time in history, Spain had been instrumental in cocaine's emergence.

Drugs were destined to dominate, control, manipulate and encourage many gangs on an international level. However, drugs, including cocaine, crack, heroin and synthetic drugs, were not the only pressing concern for gangs and gang warfare. Across the globe, kidnap, guns, money laundering, armed robbery, fraud, smuggling (including people smuggling), bikers and hi-tech crime would all, in time, play their part. Interestingly, newspaper articles reported, in the autumn of 2012, that crime had been steadily falling for the best part of 20 years, reaching its lowest levels for a quarter of a century. Personal crimes – including pickpocketing – were highlighted as being on the increase, but the number of overall crimes being reported in England and Wales had dropped to an all-time low. Figures showed that the numbers of crimes reported were a third lower than they had been in 2002–03. Crimes for murder, attempted murder and other violent crimes had dropped significantly, but personal, less violent crimes had risen by 6 per cent, according to reports. Statistics revealed that total crime had fallen since 1989, although it seems that worrying incidents of civil unrest don't really count in the findings, due to the way in which official records are compiled. While personal crimes may have increased during the early part of the 21st century, another area that appears not to feature to any extent in the figures is card fraud – yet this is one area in which gangs have "cashed-in" over recent years. The fact that crime has fallen quite so dramatically is startling, and perhaps misleading. It's true that many repeat offenders are currently in prison (prison populations are perpetually high), but news reports, particularly local bulletins, are full of gang leaders and other members being prosecuted. There are, it would appear, many willing and able to take the places of those who are incarcerated. Is it also possible that crimes are being lumped together, rather than being recorded on an individual level? For example, individual banks are included within the statistics, but victims of card fraud are not. However, the National Crime Survey – which began in 1981 – suggested, in a report from October 2012, that crime was at its lowest level since its findings were first published. On the flip side, Victim Support is still extremely busy and is aware that crime is still a very real issue for thousands of people every month. While, if the figures are accurate, it's reassuring to know that crime levels are falling significantly, at least in an official capacity, general feeling points to the fact that another important number is also falling – that is, the number of people who have confidence in the police. Many people believe that crime figures are meaningless and distorted, mainly because a large number of crimes actually go unreported. The reason for this seems to be that people don't see the point in reporting many crimes – they just don't feel that they get the support and consideration they deserve or expect, while public opinion also cites a belief that police "cherry-pick" the incidents they can, or will, deal with. But is this fair? Gangs are a powerful and dangerous backdrop to society, woven into the very fabric of everyday life, and they appear to be on the rise. While gangs led by the likes of the Krays and the Richardsons go back to a bygone era of old-fashioned values, honour, retribution mixed with loyalty and an underbelly wrapped in its own world, modern-day gangs are a mystery to many, purely because their operations are so different, widespread and far-reaching. Yes, gangs still have their territories within cities – often marked by some kind of sign – but international gangs have taken over from "local" outfits, crimes are becoming increasingly complex, and virtually anything today can be a commodity to be traded, "owned" and fought over illegally. In the mid to latter part of the 20th century, members of gangs thought themselves part of a noble profession. Perhaps now it's less defined. However, even past gangs still have their place in modern society. During their time in prison, both Ronnie and Reggie Kray were "available" on a consultancy basis. For significant "fees" they made introductions, and while cities including Manchester, Birmingham, Bristol, Sheffield, Liverpool and Glasgow (which has a long-established gang history) have come to prominence, London is still renowned as the hub for gang activity. Cities in the north, particularly in Yorkshire – such as Leeds, Bradford and Doncaster – also play their part. The nature of the drugs trade requires a far-reaching intricate web of contacts, with "big players" established in major and not-so-major cities in order for it to work. When the Krays were imprisoned in 1969, police were confident that their gangland activities had been brought to an end, but these entrepreneurs were able to establish a new criminal empire from behind bars, by implementing sponsorship-type arrangements with up-and-coming outfits who were happy to pay (large amounts of money) to be able to use the Kray name. Being a part of the Kray "Firm" would give any aspiring criminal gang a life-changing opportunity, while the twins made a fortune through drug deals, scams and robberies without implicating themselves in any way. Until the end of their lives, Ronnie and Reggie Kray were to remain pivotal in the underworld and dedicated leaders of the Firm. Even today, the Firm continues with the same values and principles that it had during the mid-1960s. Within the criminal underworld it is a trusted network, with domestic and international connections. Although drugs were a huge part of the organization's activities, there are reports that illicit drugs are now on the decline. Home Office figures, published in September 2012, showed low-level usage of drugs, including heroin, although prescribed methadone usage had increased by 0.1 per cent over the previous two years. According to the Home Office survey, 19 per cent of people aged 16–24 had used illicit drugs in the preceding 12 months. Cannabis proved the most popular drug (with around 2.3 million users), but cocaine was still high on the list, with around 700,000 having taken the drug between 2011 and 2012. While some experts cite that drugs are no longer seen as "cool" and that economic factors have had an impact on drug usage, leading to a decline, others, including some politicians, believe that drugs are just as prevalent as ever. Public opinion in some quarters states that drug usage is definitely on the increase in certain areas of the UK, while if you look at various blogs and other discussion forums on the Internet, it looks as though prescription pill-popping is big business, with a sharp rise in users, particularly in the United States. There are those that think that, just like the fall in crime figures, the fall in drug usage is distorted: do people actually admit to drug usage when surveyed by a random stranger? Many believe that drugs are actually on the increase because they're "safer" than alcohol and tobacco. When it comes to gangs, there seems to be little evidence to suggest that drugs are significantly falling in status and value. In fact, drug misuse is one of the signs cited by professionals that a child is being sexually exploited and abused by a gang. According to a report published in November 2012, thousands of children each year are abused in this way. The Office of the Children's Commissioner conducted a study, which reported that between 2010 and 2011, 16,500 children were at high risk. The two-year inquiry – the first of its kind – set out the scale of the problem, particularly in the aftermath of the Rochdale incident, where the grooming and sexual exploitation of young girls resulted in nine Asian men being jailed in May 2012. The report set out 13 factors that could indicate that children and young people were at risk of, or subject to, sexual exploitation, including drug misuse, alcohol, physical injuries and self-harming. Just three of these signs are enough to signal that the child in question is at risk. As in domestic abuse, victims of sexual exploitation and perpetrators come from all ethnic groups and different types of backgrounds, although the largest group of perpetrators identified by the report (around a third) were white. The reality is, that each year thousands of children are abducted, trafficked, beaten, threatened and raped after being drawn in by false promises by, predominantly, gangs of men (and women) who routinely fail to come to the attention of the authorities due to a lack of standardized practices and processes across police forces with regard to recording sexual offences against children by multiple perpetrators. As with many "modern" crimes, the sexual exploitation of children still has so many facets that need to be understood by those in a position to do something about it. While urgent action to stop these heinous crimes is needed, until those in authority actually know exactly what it is they're dealing with and have the resources to standardize practices across all departments, it seems likely that thousands of children will remain at risk and that many more will join them. The sharing of data is paramount for a start, yet, to date, this still doesn't happen in the way it's needed. The report identified that children as young as 11 were at risk; however, when significantly younger children go missing, there is always the question as to whether they've been abducted by a gang for sex trafficking. Little children including Sarah Payne, Ben Needham and Madeleine McCann were all thought to have been kidnapped to order at some point after their disappearance. Sarah was cruelly murdered by convicted paedophile Roy Whiting, but the whereabouts of Ben and Madeleine have never been discovered. There have been many reported sightings of both children over the years since they were abducted, but none has brought respite for their anguished parents. It is likely that they may never know what happened – which is very disturbing. Human trafficking by gangs is documented as the fastest growing criminal industry worldwide. The profits for the perpetrators go into billions of dollars. The victims of these gang-based crimes are often subjected to a life of sexual exploitation. At this point in time, the International Labour Organization estimates that around 250 million children between the ages of five and 17 are being sexually exploited following their abduction. In the UK, it's vital that the police, health authorities, councils and other related agencies work more closely together, alongside local communities, to stamp out this criminal behaviour.

Trying to tackle the problems related to gangs is the Serious Organised Crime Agency (SOCA), established in 2006 through the merger of the National Crime Squad and the National Criminal Intelligence Service as well as the National Hi-Tech Crime Unit, sections of HM Revenue & Customs (HMRC) responsible for drug trafficking, and the departments of the Immigration Service which work against organized immigration crimes. SOCA organizations were further merged into a larger, more powerful National Crime Agency in 2013. Sponsored by, but independent of, the Home Office, SOCA – sometimes referred to as the British FBI by domestic newspapers – devotes 40 per cent of its time and resources to tackling drug trafficking, 25 per cent to organized immigration crime, 15 per cent to other organized crime, 10 per cent to fraud, and the remaining 10 per cent to supporting other agencies. Despite budget cuts across the agency in recent years, one independent area of SOCA is the Child Exploitation and Online Protection Centre (CEOP), which opened a CEOP Academy as a centre of excellence. The CEOP also works alongside New Scotland Yard's hi-tech Child Abuse Investigation Command. SOCA confirms that most gangs operate in today's society in London, Manchester and Liverpool, as well as across the West Midlands, the north and south coasts. Street gangs concentrated in these areas – alongside gangs in Glasgow – are responsible for more than two-thirds of firearms-related murders in the UK, but more urban areas, including Leicester, are also suffering from the emergence of gang-style organized crimes. Many of these crimes, as already discussed, are related to drugs and exploitation, however, firearms and prostitution are also major players in this underbelly of modern life. Gang influences from the United States have infiltrated the fabric of gang society in the UK, and even the US Crips and Bloods have developed branches in the British Isles. Today, in Manchester, gangs like the Old Trafford Cripz and Moss Side Bloods operate with US-influenced identification, including graffiti tags, hand signs, tattoos and colours. Ironically, the first gang capital was originally London, before gangs expanded into cities like New York, Los Angeles, Chicago, and into South America, including Mexico City. Gang culture has been around for more than 100 years. Some of the earliest gangs in Manchester sprang up in the mid-19th century in the slum dwellings of the city, although gangs had mostly disappeared there by the beginning of the early 1900s. The Penny Mobs in Glasgow were first recorded in the press in the 1870s, although the city's history of gangs can be traced back to the 18th century. Up to the 1920s these Scottish gangs were more about fighting than they were about crime, but within a decade that began to change, and by the 1930s gang violence was widespread. Despite the changes in gangs from the Thirties and through their heyday in the 1960s and what they've become today, with regard to the issues that surround gangs and the organized crime, many of the reports documented in earlier centuries read quite similarly to today's newspaper articles and commentaries. Perhaps not much has changed. This book seeks to cover archived newspaper articles on gang organizations in the UK and further afield, from the beginning of the 20th century to the present day.

Notorious Gangs of the 20th and 21st Centuries

In Glasgow, the Thompson Gang ruled the city for three decades from the 1970s to the 1990s. Their "Godfather", Arthur Thompson, began his criminal empire as a council estate moneylender. Those who failed to pay their debts were "crucified" by being nailed to doors and furniture, while protection rackets and forays into the drug trade soon followed. Although a feared man of violence, there were rivals out for Thompson's blood. In 1966 he escaped death when a bomb exploded under his car, but his mother-in-law was killed. The following week, Thompson spotted two rival gangsters he suspected of the bomb attack in a van. He forced the vehicle off the road with his car. The van hit a lamp post and both men were killed. Twenty-five years later, in 1991, Thompson's son, Arthur Jr, known as "Fatboy", was shot dead outside the family home. A rival gangland figure, Paul Ferris, was arrested for the shooting. On the day of Fatboy's funeral, the bodies of two of Ferris' friends, Robert Glover and Joe "Bananas" Hanlon, were found dumped by the route of the funeral procession. Both had been shot in the head and up the anus.

Colombia also had its issues in the 20th century. By 1980, the cocaine smuggled out of the country had overtaken coffee as

Columbia's number one export. The illegal trade was controlled by a ruthless collection of gangsters, armed with military weapons and based in the country's second-largest city, Medellín. At its height, the Medellín Cartel was shipping 15 tons of cocaine per day (worth US$60m) around the world. The gang, led by Juan Pablo Escobar and "Uncle" Joe Ochoa, were ruthless in eliminating anyone who tried to stop them. They assassinated more than 30 leading judges, police officers and politicians who opposed them. They even killed 110 innocents when they bombed a plane in an attempt to murder presidential candidate César Trujillo – who was not even on the flight. In the end, with the backing of undercover US Special Forces, the Columbian Government cracked down on the Cartel. Escobar and Ochoa were hunted down and killed by police. The Cartel's grip had been broken.

In North America, charismatic but psychotic hippie Charles Manson gathered a group of male and female followers around him in California in 1969. He called them the Manson Family.

Manson had studied the occult and convinced his followers of his Helter Skelter theory: that a coming race war would end the world. In August 1969, he led his heavily armed followers to a ranch near Los Angeles. Here they found actress Sharon Tate. Her husband, film director Roman Polanski, was in the UK on business at the time. Tate, who was eight months pregnant, was with three friends, Jay Sebring, Wojciech Frykowski and Abigail Folger. Manson and his followers massacred them all in an orgy of stabbing and shooting. The following day, Manson and his "disciples" murdered another couple, Rosemary and Leno LaBianca, in their LA home. Police found Manson had used his victims' blood to scrawl the words "Helter Skelter" on the door of a fridge. Manson was denied parole for the 12th time in April 2012 and will remain in a Californian state prison until he is at least 92 years old.

In the UK, around the same time that Manson was active, the Kray twins ruled London. Boxing brothers Ronald ("Ronnie") and Reginald ("Reggie") Kray led a criminal gang that dominated the East End of London by fear throughout the 1950s and 1960s. Despite being involved in armed robbery, arson, protection rackets and violent assaults – which included torture and murder – through their status as nightclub owners the twins mixed with the likes of Judy Garland, Frank Sinatra and Diana Dors, to become celebrities in their own right. Beneath all the glamour of the Swinging Sixties, however, there lurked a cold brutality. Ronnie Kray shot and killed rival George Cornell in the Blind Beggar pub in Whitechapel in March 1966. Then, in late 1967, the gang lured minor associate, Jack "the Hat" McVitie, to a basement flat in Stoke Newington, where Reggie tried to shoot him. The gun failed to discharge, so, while Ronnie held McVitie in a bear hug, Reggie was handed a carving knife with which he stabbed the man repeatedly in the face, stomach and neck. In 1969 the Krays were both sentenced to life imprisonment, with a non-parole period of 30 years for the murders of Cornell and McVitie; the longest sentences ever passed at the Old Bailey for murder.

Bisexual Ronnie, who was thought to suffer from paranoid schizophrenia, died in Broadmoor Hospital, Crowthorne, in 1995. In August 2000, at the age of 67, Reggie was released from Norfolk's Wayland Prison on compassionate grounds. He was suffering from inoperable bladder cancer and died in his sleep on 1st October that same year.

Bikers, particularly in Australia, New Zealand and the United States, are also renowned for their gangland activities and culture. America's Aryan Brotherhood are believed to have begun with an Irish–American biker gang serving time in St Quentin jail in 1964. Up until then, prisons in the USA had been segregated, but when the system disbanded prisoners started to group together on racial lines. The FBI lists the Aryan Brotherhood (AB) as one of America's most powerful organized crime groups. At first, the AB only attacked and murdered black people, but, by the 1980s, the Brotherhood had expanded its activities into large-scale financially motivated organized crime. This included the interstate movement of stolen cars, motorbikes and industrial machinery, armed robbery and hitmen for hire. Although the AB make up just 1 per cent of the USA's prison population, Federal authorities say that the gang is responsible for 21 per cent of all prison murders.

In 2002, the FBI launched a nationwide drive against the Brotherhood: 29 of its leaders were arrested, while bosses Tyler "The Hulk" Bingham and Barry Mill were jailed for life without parole for a series of murders.

On the other side of the world, organized crime in Japan is

dominated by the Yakuza families, also known as Boryokudan, which literally means violence group. There are three main families, the largest of which is the Yamaguchi Gumi, from the city of Kobe. Yakuza members are expected to adhere to many rituals. Ranks inside the organization are displayed by complex tattoos; some of them are full body artwork, applied by using the most painful, traditional methods of ink and bamboo needles. If a Yakuza member offends his bosses, his honour code dictates that he must sever the top joint of his finger with a knife in the presence of his gang boss, who is presented with the digit as an apology. Yakuza gangs control the booming sex trade in Japan's red-light districts. They run protection and blackmail rackets involving many businesses, and firms often include pay-off money to the Yakuza in their annual accounts. It is thought that the gangs have penetrated the banking world. After a recent property crash, in 2012, several bank managers were assassinated, apparently as Yakuza retribution for bad investment advice.

Another biker gang that has caused widespread fear is the Hell's Angels. The origins of the Hell's Angels can be traced back to California in 1948, but, since then, the movement has spread worldwide, with an estimated 250,000 members. Although the Hell's Angels describes itself as a motorcycle club, the US Justice Department and the FBI describe it as a "major organized crime group". The gang is divided into chapters, usually based on towns or cities, and it has a number of rituals. In the USA, members must be white, have no convictions for sex offences against children, and must own an American-made motorbike, usually a Harley-Davidson. Full members are allowed to wear the distinctive, winged death's-head patch on their jackets. In the USA, Canada, Sweden, Germany and Australia (where they clamped down heavily on biker gangs in 2012), police have special units just to deal with such gangs. In the UK, in 2007, Gerry Tobin, a Hell's Angel, was shot dead, as he rode his bike along the M40, by a rival gang member after a rock festival. A party, intended to settle scores between rival British Angel chapters, ended in a bloodbath near Reading in 1980, with two murders and a dozen more victims seriously injured in battles with knives, axes and sawn-off shotguns.

The Yardies originated from the slums of Jamaica. Yardie gangs emerged in the 1960s, spawning powerful groups known as posses – the two most powerful and influential of these being the Spangler and Shower posses. Yardie gangs began to surface in Britain in the early 1980s In areas of London, Birmingham and Bristol, where communities, originally from Jamaica, had settled. These gangs fought each other over control of the drugs trade, prostitution and shebeens – illegal drinking and gambling clubs. One of the most notorious Yardie gang incidents in Britain happened in 1993, when posse members shot dead DJ William Danso at a house in Clapham, London. The gang then gunned down Patrick Dunne, an unarmed community police constable, who was passing on his bicycle. Feared Yardie gunman Gary "Tyson" Nelson was jailed for life for the murders.

The two most notorious American street gangs are the Crips, founded in 1969 in South Central Los Angeles, and the Bloods. The Crips formed through the amalgamation of several local street gangs under the leadership of Raymond Washington and Stanley "Tookie" Williams. In reaction to their dominance, a breakaway group of Crips, known as the Piru Street Gang from Compton, formed the Bloods. It is a popular misconception that Crips gangs feud only with Bloods, whereas, in reality, different sets of Crips often feud with each other over turf and local rivalries. Extreme violence is common, with LA gang squad officers estimating that there have been more than 5,000 murders involving the groups over the past 20 years. The gangs have ritualized recognition symbols, including tattoos, music, hand signs, language, graffiti and dress codes. Crips wear blue, while Bloods can be identified by the colour red. In the early 1980s, Crips sets began distributing crack cocaine in Los Angeles. Due to its profitability, this distribution quickly spread nationwide, thereby attracting new members. Police estimate the total membership of both groups of street gangs to be around 50,000 across the United States.

Meanwhile, back in Europe, the Cosa Nostra was founded in Sicily in the 19th century as a powerful crime group who operated under an honour code governed by *Omerta* – the rule of silence. When thousands of Sicilians emigrated to the United States in the early 20th century, they took their traditions with them, leading to the modern-day Italian/American crime Mafia families that have dominated American organized crime ever since. In Sicily, the Cosa Nostra remains a powerful influence even now, with many businesses and wealthy individuals subject to extortion. An ongoing Government drive to stamp out the organization in Sicily has led to a "war", with many Mafia figures having been jailed, but, in reprisals, more than 200 prosecutors, police chiefs, judges and politicians have been assassinated by bomb or bullet.

An article in the *Mirror* outlined how gangs have "infested" Britain's streets for more than 300 years, but that those of the 21st century had multiplied as never before. Scotland Yard estimated that as many as 400 separate drug gangs operated in London alone in 2003. At the bottom of the pyramid were the teenage gangs, with members as young as 10, based on housing estates. Members "graduate" to form more serious crime gangs, becoming involved in the theft of high-value cars, jewellery snatches and other valuables, while attacks on wealthy suburban homes where gangs literally crashed through front doors to terrorize families and grab whatever they could were on the increase. Running parallel with this are the crime groups, who sometimes have political links in their own countries. At the top of the heap, sit the cream of villains, from several racial backgrounds, who control large-scale operations such as drug smuggling and protection rackets involving pubs, clubs, restaurants and bars. In a gripping article, the *Mirror* took a look at the gangs who were terrorizing British streets in the early years of the 21st century. It began with Manchester, where gangs included the Gooch – spawned from the original Gooch Close Gang, the Doddington, the Pitt Bull Crew, the Longsight Soldiers and the Longsight Crew. At the height of their power, there were 500 members among all the city's gangs. Drugs and murder were high on the agenda for these gangs. In 2002, the leader of the Pitt Bull Crew, Thomas Pitt, was given a life sentence for murder and 20 years for three attempted assassinations, racketeering and drugs charges. A total of 13 members of this gang were sentenced to more than 170 years in jail, plus three life sentences. They were linked to at least three murders.

Pitt, 24, headed the gang, and routinely walked the streets armed with a MAC-10 sub-machine gun, complete with silencer. He formed the gang in memory of his dead brother, Ray Pitt, who was shot dead outside a nightclub on New Year's Eve 1996. Pitt employed a team of enforcers to carry heroin, cocaine and cannabis around Manchester's infamous "gang triangle" of Longsight, Moss Side and Hulme. His crew included boys as young as 14, who cruised around on mountain bikes. Pitt gunned down rival drug dealer Marcus Greenidge, 21, as he loitered on a grass verge in Longsight in September 2000. A police source said: "While the gangs were originally fighting over control of the drugs market, it is now much more about territory."

In Liverpool, gangs include Curtis Warren, the Fitzgibbons, the Clarkes, and the Lawlors, where each is run by a number of family members and associates. The crimes of choice in Liverpool involve drugs, security and extortion. The city's most notorious gangster, Curtis Warren, served a 12-year sentence in

Holland for smuggling cocaine worth £125 million. In addition to the 1997 sentence, he received four years for killing a man in prison and an extra six years for failing to pay a multi-million-pound fine to the Dutch authorities. But Warren is still believed to be running his crime empire and is said to be worth more than £100 million. He is also thought to earn a fortune from 200 domestic properties and commercial property.

Warren's arch-rivals were the Fitzgibbons. When father-of-three David Ungi, 36 – a Fitzgibbon relative – was gunned down on 1st May 1995, it triggered a bloodbath on the streets. It is widely believed that Warren sanctioned the murder, which began a street war that saw 44 shootings in the months after Ungi's death. Brothers Ian and Jason Fitzgibbons remained gang leaders, but, in May 1998, police launched Operation Black to topple them. In July 2000, Jason and Ian pleaded guilty to conspiracy to supply heroin and were jailed for eight and seven years respectively. In 2001, the Clarke gang, from Netherley, flexed its muscles when Stephen Lawlor, one of Warren's friends, died in a hail of bullets as he left a party. Soldier Peter Clarke, 22, was given a life sentence for his murder. Four months later, Clarke's brother Ian, 32, was shot as he sat in a car outside a pub. The feud continued when, weeks later, Stephen Lawlor's brother Anthony, 45, was chased by four assassins and shot dead in front of his mum. No one has been charged with these last two killings.

In Birmingham, the story is much the same. The gangs include the Burger Bar Boys or Burgers, Johnson Crew or Jonnies, the Champagne Crew, the Rally Close Crew and the Badder Boys. Activities in the West Midlands involve murder, drugs, protection and theft. The Burgers formed in the late 1980s and were named after a takeaway; they are said to be led by S1, alias Donald Somers, who served three years for drugs offences. The gang was thought to be responsible for the New Year's Day murders of Charlene Ellis and Letisha Shakespeare, and of Johnson Crew member Christopher Clarke, 22, in March 2000. Donald Somers was investigated in connection with the murder of Corey Wayne Allen, who was shot with his own gun in Handsworth in 2000. The case was dropped through lack of evidence. It was also rumoured that Allen, himself a Burger Bar Boy and suspected killer, had turned police informer and was executed by his own gang. Yardie gangster Whitcliffe Brissett, 33, found dead in a Ford Sierra in Smethwick, West Midlands, in September 2000, was said to have shot himself when his gun accidently went off. However, the coroner was unconvinced and recorded an open verdict. Brissett had been charged with the 1995 attempted murder of William Marr, who refused to give evidence against Brissett and was jailed for contempt of court in February 1996. The Johnson Crew, who was trying to wrestle the drugs trade from the Burger and invade its territory, was suspected of the murder in 2002 of Burger Bar Boy Yohanne Martin, 24. Two teenage girls appeared in court in connection with his killing in 2003. In 1996, Burger Boy Jason Wharton was shot dead in Handsworth. Several

Johnson Crew members were jailed for terms ranging from life to five years after witnesses gave evidence behind bulletproof screens (while wearing disguises).

London has a long history of gang warfare, but in the 21st century the gangs comprise the Chinese Triads, Chinese Snakehead, Vietnamese gangs, Turkish and Kurdish gangs, Nigerian and Ghanaian fraud gangs, Jamaican gangs and black posses, as well as Balkan gangs, former Communist Bloc gangs, Asian gangs, Irish gangs and others. Activities are varied and differ depending on where the gang originally comes from. Chinese Triads are involved in loan sharking, extortion, gambling and fraud, while the Chinese Snakehead concentrates on smuggling and illegal immigrants. The Vietnamese gangs are similar to the Chinese, while Turkish and Kurdish gangs are mainly involved in drugs. Nigerian and Ghanaian gangs work in fraud; Jamaican and black posses are involved in drugs, prostitution, theft, robbery and organized car theft; while Balkan gangs prefer smuggling, particularly women for prostitution, drugs, guns and illegal immigrants, and are involved in contract killings. Gangs run by the former Communist Bloc are responsible for trading in women for vice and pornography, extortion, importing counterfeit goods and exporting stolen luxury cars, while Asian gangs concentrate their activities on fraud, drugs, extortion, robbery and smuggling illegal immigrants. The Irish gangs are notorious for armed robbery, drugs and protection.

Snakeheads organized the smuggling of illegal immigrants

in which 58 of their "clients" died from asphyxiation in a truck stopped at Dover docks. Turkish syndicates, many Kurdish, have an iron grip on Britain's £100 million per year heroin trade. About 50 rival gang members fought a street battle with guns and knives in Stoke Newington in November 2003, leaving one dead and 20 seriously hurt. Police said that Turkish and Jamaican gangs were starting up partnerships in London. It was estimated that Jamaican gangs were responsible for 500 murders and 5,000 other gun attacks during the 10 years up to 2003. Asian drug and protection gangs were linked to four murders in two years in Southall. A pub was firebombed and a boy of 17 was suspected of two contract hits. Asian gangs in East London were said to be involved in worldwide credit fraud. Nigerian and Ghanaian fraud gangs had an annual take of £500 million. A drugs war between two Irish gangs in 2002 led to four contract killings. Also in 2002, Irish brothers Sean and Vincent Bradish, from Brent, were jailed for 22 years each for more than 30 armed robberies.

The north of the UK is also no stranger to gang-related crime. Although the area is smaller than that of a massive city like London, the gang culture in Tyneside is no less worrying. The Convoys, the Sayers and the Firm operate in the north, with activities including armed robbery, abduction, blackmail and drugs. Patrick Conroy was once one of the most wanted men in Britain. He went on the run after escaping custody and was eventually arrested in Spain. On his return, his trial heard how one of his rivals screamed in agony as the roots of his teeth were exposed through torture.

Conroy was found guilty of abducting and torturing a suspected member of another gang in Newcastle's tough West End. He was jailed for 11 years in 1995, but was closely monitored by the Home Office while behind bars because of his extensive underworld contacts across Europe. At one time, the three Sayers brothers were serving a total of 37 years behind bars. While they were inside, their father, John Sayer Sr was shot in the face in an apparent gangland hit. John Henry Jr was jailed in February 1990 for plotting an armed raid on Pritchard's security firm in Gateshead, where masked robbers with shotguns and sledgehammers smashed in to steal £400,000 in wages. Sayers has always protested his innocence, but failed in an appeal to overturn his sentence. In 1997, younger brothers Stephen and Michael were jailed for 10 and 12 years respectively for a £50,000 plot to blackmail a local businessman.

In 2005, it was reported that gangs were involved in a "jail reign of terror". Gangs were bringing drugs and violence into Britain's largest jail, it was claimed. Chief inspector of prisons, Anne Owers, said guards had been overwhelmed by an "imported" street gang culture. And some officers were turning a blind eye. Owers' report found bullied inmates living in fear at HMP Liverpool. More than 90 per cent felt unsafe on one wing, 56 per cent said it was easy to get illegal drugs and more than 30 per cent of drug tests were positive. Ms Owers said: "It was clear the gang culture of the streets had infiltrated the prison resulting in easy access to drugs and in bullying." But it didn't stop there. Another report, carried out in 2005, claimed that gangs were ruling in one in five schools across the UK. Gang culture was rife in 20 per cent of schools, the shock report stated. Nearly 40 per cent of these schools had a problem with pupils carrying weapons. A study by the Office of Standards in Education found that children's behaviour was getting more out of control. Its report said: "The behaviour of some pupils, usually boys, remains a serious concern for many schools." Drug abuse was a "daily challenge", it claimed. Only 68 per cent of secondary schools rated pupils' behaviour as "good or better". The report said: "Gang culture was perceived as widespread in one in five secondary schools visited." It said extreme violence was rare but added: "Incidents of verbal and physical abuse aimed at peers is a problem in most schools." The most common form of poor behaviour was persistent low-level disruption of lessons, which wore down staff and interrupted learning. However, there was anger at the Department of Education at the tone of the report, which was based on visits to just 15 schools. It was felt that a very small minority reported a growing perception in gang culture.

Former gang member Stanley "Tookie" Williams was to be executed on death row in December 2005. Williams faced execution for the murder of four people he robbed in Los Angeles 26 years earlier. The Supreme Court had thrown out his final appeal without hearing it, and it fell to Governor Arnold Schwarzenegger to decide the convicted killer's fate. Williams had his story made into a film, Redemption, released in 2004. He said he was a changed man after 24 years in tough San Quentin jail, and it was reported that he counselled gang members on how to turn their lives around. He was nominated five times for the Nobel Peace Prize. It was true that many preachers, politicians and law enforcement officers talked often about stopping gang violence, but, in reality, they had no experience of how to. Williams was different. Williams was the founder of the most well-known gang in history – the leader of LA's feared Crips gang. He was eventually given four death sentences for murder in 1981. Even in jail, Williams continued his gang activity and got six-and-a-half years in solitary confinement. But, in February 1997, he wrote an open apology. He said he regretted his former gangster lifestyle and vowed to spend the rest of his life working towards solutions. He wrote nine children's books aimed at stopping them joining gangs. However, Williams failed to win clemency and was executed on 13th December 2005.

Children's and youth involvement in gang-related crimes did not improve into 2006. At least one child a day was charged with a firearms crime, claimed a probe by the *Mirror*. The youth gun culture had exploded, according to the newspaper in December that year. Nearly 800 youngsters – some as young as 10 – had appeared in court on gun charges since the start of 2005. A further 2,200 were arrested. Sixteen teenagers, including a 14-year-old, had been charged with gun murder. The *Mirror's* investigation revealed, for the first time, the full scale of the problem that was claiming more and more young lives. Experts blamed the growing gun and drug gang culture. They also pointed to the sinister "grooming" of children by adult criminals, who got the kids to keep weapons so they themselves did not get caught.

Gangsta rap music was also cited as being to blame for the glamorization of guns and violence, claimed the report. The figures – obtained under the Freedom of Information Act – could, in reality, have been even worse, because 11 police forces did not supply the newspaper with statistics for the report. The trend was all the more worrying because, in general, gun crime was actually down. In London, for example, it had fallen 24 per cent in a year. The Met's Operation Trident, which investigates shootings in the black community, had at this point launched a campaign targeting 11 to 16 year olds. Until April 2005, the squad had not charged anybody under 20 with murder. But between this date and December 2006 it had charged 16 teenagers (including the 14-year-old). Inspector Steve Tyler said: "The trend is the victims are younger and the murderers are younger. There is a subculture of young people who are out of control. The way they live their lives is not like us and it can easily lead to guns."

Patsy McKie, of Mothers Against Violence – whose son Dorrie, 20, was shot dead in Hulme, Manchester, in 1999 – said: "This problem has not been well known and people need to hear about it. We need to move people into action. Adults have to take responsibility because somewhere along the line we have become oblivious to what is going on around us." Other victims at the time included Jessie James, 15, killed in Moss

Side, Manchester, in September 2005, and Nathan Williams, 17, shot dead in Nottingham just days later. The problem was not confined to cities. Ten-year-olds were arrested in Norfolk, Thames Valley, Surrey and Hertfordshire. Bedfordshire police cautioned a 13-year-old girl for carrying a gun and charged a 12-year-old boy with possessing a gun with intent to cause fear of violence. Supt Adrian Bowers, West Midlands' lead gun crime officer, believed primary school children should be educated. He said: "We need to go into schools, talk to children of 10 or under and warn them of the dangers of guns and gangs." One youth worker, Uanu Seshmi, director of a group which helps teenagers in London escape gang culture, blamed "Fagin-style" crooks. He believed that these criminals were corrupting youngsters, while the influence of gangsta rap was also behind the huge rise in kids' gun crime. He said: "Adults are exploiting young people by giving them guns to take from A to B. They know if the kids are caught they will get away with an Asbo. The youngsters accept it because they believe the only way to be recognized as men is to carry or use firearms. This is fuelled by gangsta rappers who glamorize gun culture."

By 2007, knives were on the increase too. The number of knife thugs on the streets soared nearly sevenfold because of growing gang warfare. In 1996, just 890 youths were convicted for carrying blades in public. But, by 2006, there were nearly seven times as many at 5,967 – a 569 per cent increase. There was also a 60 per cent rise in youths sentenced over carrying other brutal weapons such as clubs and knuckledusters – up from 3,545 to 5,689. Opposition politicians blamed the trend on increasingly violent teenage gangs. Lib Dem Home Affairs spokesman, Jeremy Browne, warned: "Britain's growing gang culture is threatening the safety of many young people. Knives kill far more people in Britain than guns. Knives are deadly weapons, not fashion accessories, and need to be treated accordingly."

Police and the Home Office claimed the rise in sentences was partly down to a tougher crackdown in nailing more perpetrators; however, insiders privately feared that the five-year minimum jail term for carrying guns had merely seen criminals switch to blades. Ministers had doubled the maximum term for having a knife, but were thought to be reluctant to set a minimum, fearing an explosion in convictions would overwhelm already packed jails. The then home secretary, John Reid, admitted gangs had a "devastating" effect but said the key was better education and communities working with police. He thought that Britain had the ability to make cities safer – but did this happen? By the time Britain reached the end of the first decade of the 21st century, a poll indicated that nearly half of all adults were afraid to go out at night due to increased numbers of teenage gangs. No wonder, in 2007, two teenagers were arrested in connection with the shooting and death of 11-year-old Rhys Jones.

London alone had seen at least six teenagers killed in shootings between February and August 2007. Seventeen had been murdered in total that same year. So was it anarchy in the

UK, or were some youngsters being given a bad name? Sixteen-year-old Spencer Hardcastle from Bradford, West Yorkshire, explained that many groups of mates out and about were quite rowdy. It would be natural to think they were up to no good. "We mess around and our clothes may not be exactly to your taste," he said, "Chances are, we're just on our way to the cinema or bowling." However, that doesn't stop worried people from crossing to the other side of the road when they see Spencer and his mates. The group was not allowed to go into certain shops together, due to the retailer's fear of trouble, and when they're spoken to no one looks the lads in the eye. Apparently, that's what being a teenager is about in the 21st century. It is thought that most adults think all teenagers are looking for trouble, yet Spencer says, "We just want to buy a Big Mac."

"I don't like being called a yob because I try my best to behave. But many people have a stereotypical view of teenagers, which most of the time, is completely untrue and unfair. I like to hang around with my friends, but I'm not in a gang." Spencer explained that many teenagers don't belong to gangs and that they were just as shocked to hear about the death of Rhys Jones as anyone else. But, he points out that, unlike adults, he doesn't have a fear of going out because there's the possibility of death on the streets. He said: "I know there is more good than bad in the world." But he was quick to point out that he knew he was lucky. His parents had encouraged him to do well, had supported him and gave him rules to live by. It is widely recognized that most of the young people who get into trouble have never known what it is like to have strict but loving parents, and often don't have role models. Spencer believed that ASBOs didn't work, because the youngsters who got them didn't have rules and values in the first place. An ASBO would not change their ways.

Spencer's protestations that many teenagers are not part of a gang and that young people are not all out to cause trouble are true. But, in 2007, one in 10 teenagers said they had carried a knife and 6 per cent claimed to have carried a gun. How true these figures are is hard to prove, but almost half of 15-year-olds had been involved in a violent fight. Two out of three 15-year-olds had been drunk, while 86 per cent of under 18-year-olds had drunk alcohol. More than 10 per cent of 13-year-olds and 25 per cent of 15-year-olds smoked something at least once a week, while over a quarter spent more than four hours a day watching TV. One in three youngsters had had sex by the age of 15.

The tragic death of 11-year-old Rhys Jones in Liverpool was met with a wall of silence. Yet, according to one witness, at least 15 young people had a good view of the killer who gunned down the child. The witness spoke out as police tried to break down the wall of silence hampering the inquiry into the murder. The witness said the hooded teenage killer was just 10 feet from a crowd of boys and girls who watched the horror unfold. The youngsters would have clearly seen the gunman as he shot the small Everton fan in the back of the neck. The witness stated to press how sickening it was that none of these youngsters had come forward to help the child.

On 24th August 2007, the street name of the alleged killer was posted on the video of the Croxteth Crew brandishing guns, posted on YouTube. A message that accompanied the name asked the alleged killer to hand himself in. Police were said to be investigating, but they were disappointed by the number of calls they had in relation to the murder. The witness who claimed that many people would be able to identify the murderer ran over to help Rhys as he lay dying in the car park of the Fir Tree pub in Croxteth Park, Liverpool. He had been shot by a lad on a BMX bike, who stopped for a few seconds after the shooting before riding off. All the youngsters present would have had a clear view of his face.

There were those who declared that the fact these youngsters wouldn't come forward was a sign of just how out of control the gang culture had become as the 21st century took shape. However, a major study conducted by a leading criminologist had found that nearly half of teenage gang members are bullied into joining. A fifth said they had been "reluctant" to sign up. One boy of 15 said he had been beaten up and his sister, aged 14, raped, when he refused to get involved in a gang and commit robbery for members. Another teenage gunman wept with fear as he was challenged to pull the trigger of a gun and shoot someone. A boy who witnessed it said: "He was crouched in the corner crying because he brought the gun out to protect himself and he was challenged so he pulled the trigger, he didn't want to pull the trigger."

Dr John Pitts of Bedfordshire University and the Youth Offending Team in Waltham Forest, East London, interviewed 59 teenagers for the most detailed analysis, at the time, of British gang culture. The 25 "gang-affiliated" youngsters who took part said they joined to avoid becoming a victim. One mum told the team: "I ask you to take your children into the jungle and then make you responsible for making sure they don't get eaten." Dr Pitts said some kids joined up because a crew from a rival neighbourhood would target them even if they were not in a gang. Once in, many are too scared to leave because they will lose the protection from rival gangs and face reprisals from former friends. Some were happy to stay because they gained status and money. Dr Pitts concluded that youngsters join gangs because of where they live rather than who they are. His report said: "One of the more sinister aspects of gang culture in the borough is the apparent determination of some gang members to exert control over the other residents in the territories they claim as their own." Commander Sean Sawyer, the then head of Scotland Yard's Violent Crime Directorate, said neighbourhood crews also used sexual violence as an everyday tool for "initiation, for enforcement, or for retribution".

At the same time, it was mooted that Rhys Jones could have been killed by one of the hundreds of guns smuggled into Britain from Eastern Europe. The UK was swamped with pistols bought in Russia and converted in countries such as Lithuania. Experts had little doubt that the source of many deadly weapons was Eastern

Europe, where CS and flare guns cost as little as £10 and could later be altered to fire bullets. They were then smuggled into Britain, often through the Channel Tunnel, and sold to gangsters for up to £1,500. The most popular was the Baikal, according to Britain's top forensic firearms analyst, Mark Mastaglio. He said there was a glut of the weapons in cities including Liverpool, London, Manchester and Birmingham. Since 2003, his team had examined more than 200 Baikals for the police, and identified a further 400 from bullets and cartridges found at crime scenes. Mastaglio said: "Baikals are the biggest problem. We started to see them in substantial numbers [in 2004] and they are still coming. They are the most commonly-used hand gun." In February 2007, two men, one a Lithuanian, were jailed for a total of 27 years in London for dealing in converted Baikals. A month earlier, three Lithuanians were jailed for a total of 32 years.

In 2008, the then home secretary, Jacqui Smith, warned that British gang members were beginning to "ape" the terrifying tactics of vicious American gangs. Smith declared that there was increasing evidence that gangs were wearing "colours" to show allegiance – just like rival LA gangsters, such as the Crips and the Bloods – and using graffiti "tags" to mark territory and warn off outsiders. Smith said that some elements of gang culture tended to come from the United States. In an exclusive interview with the *Mirror*, Smith said that gang members were getting younger, with teens of 14 involved in violence – partly due to tough action by police against older gangsters. But she said it meant families, especially mums, had an extra responsibility to stop teens getting dragged in. She cited that it was time to find alternatives to gangs and ways of allowing people to come out of a gang lifestyle. She said that the warning signs were increasing trouble at school, different clothes or spending time with new groups of people. However, Smith also recognized that people needed to feel confident that they didn't need to carry guns and knives. The home secretary was speaking from Birmingham in March 2008 at the start of a month-long crackdown. She vowed there would be more street searches using metal detectors, and more undercover policing. But she also wanted more "street pastor" patrols in UK cities. Trialled in Birmingham and London, the pastors are church and community volunteers who patrol gang hotspots at night. With police backup, they can mediate between rival gangs and try to talk to troubled youngsters in danger of getting into gangs. Two pupils had turned to gangs to settle a score until a mediator got them together to sort out their problems. Smith said that when there was no mediator, the situation could descend into serious violence and weapons could be involved. Smith also launched a National Ballistics Intelligence register, similar to a DNA database. The register was designed to record forensics from all guns and bullets used in crimes and find links within two days – something that had previously taken eight weeks.

Later in 2008, Britain's most senior policeman urged all parents to ask their children if they were part of the gang culture carrying knives. Youth murders and stabbings were on the increase and Sir Ian Blair wanted each and every parent to "join the fight" against these crimes. He called on parents to play their part in ending the menace – and insisted their tough love could help make the streets safe for the young again. As his plea was broadcast, it was revealed that a boy aged 12 was being quizzed over the killing of a teenager – and a boy of 11 had been charged with trying to rob a nine-year-old girl at knifepoint. He pointed out that parents had the right to demand to know if their children were carrying weapons. He wanted parents to get through to them that, if they were, they were putting themselves at significant risk. In 2008, attacks by youngsters were soaring. There were 56,000 violent attacks compared with 34,000 in 2003. The wounds that brutally murdered 17-year-old Amar Aslam, from Yorkshire, received were so severe that it took hours to identify his body. A postmortem found that he died of head injuries in a "sustained" and "brutal" attack. Police arrested seven people including boys aged 12, 13 and 15, and a 20-year-old. One MP, Shahid Malik, who lived just minutes from the murder scene, said: "We often band together these terrible attacks as being racially motivated. More often than not, it is just young people who have got involved in a culture where they feel violence is acceptable, either as an offence or in defence."

Amar's murder was thought to have taken place amid running battles between gangs. Julie Bushby of the Moorside Tenants and Residents Association said: "They call themselves the Dewsbury

Moor Crew ... People get territorial. They see what they think are the border of their area and you get a gang forming." Locals said known gangs in the area included the West Town Warriors, the Pilgrims and the Ravey Terror Squad. One woman said that youths liked to style themselves as gangsters: "They go on about guns, wave £50 notes about ... think they're big men." The boy that tried to rob the nine-year-old girl of her Nintendo DS games console by holding a pocket knife to her face was thought to belong to the Grey Gang, who were accused of terrorizing children in Walthamstow, East London. At the same time, a gang-related attack on two men in Bradford took place – one man died – while in Bromley, Greater London, two men were left fighting for their lives when two gangs clashed in a drugs row in a local pub.

In 2011, the story was worse. A terrifying arsenal of pistols, sub-machine guns and ammo was found stashed under the bed of a nine-year-old boy. A girl of five was shot among the sweets and greetings cards in a London shop, and paramedics feared they were being shot at as they desperately tried to save a young man's life. This was how gun crime had manifested itself by the second decade of the 21st century. In mid-April 2011, the blue-and-white police tape marked out the site of yet another shooting. The tape fluttered around the scene of a fatal attack at Clapham in the South London borough of Lambeth. Just two miles from where Thusha Kamaleswaran, aged five, was shot in a Stockwell newsagent's five days before, the attack in Clapham was violent and terrifying. Paramedics trying to save Isaiah Bovell's life thought they were being shot at when their ambulance window shattered. The 21-year-old victim had to be abandoned. By the time the 999 crew returned, he had died of a wound to the head. His devastated girlfriend insisted that he was not a gang member. One local retailer remarked that they were frightened to open their shop at night, but had no choice. They claimed that gang violence was getting worse. Despite the properties across the road costing up to £500,000, and affluent Clapham Common being less than a mile away, the locals spoke in hushed tones of a vicious turf war between gangs. It was revealed that up to 50 rival groups were operating in the area. The police Territorial Support Group was called in to protect locals from the gangs' tit-for-tat attacks.

Close to the scene of the shooting of the five-year-old girl, leaflets were distributed to local residents warning them not to co-operate with Operation Trident – who investigate shootings in the black community. The paper said: "The police are not your friend. Don't be deceived by promises of anonymity, protection and rewards. They will say and do anything to make you snitch, then destroy your life."

Two men were jailed in April 2011 for killing 16-year-old Agnes Sina-Inakoju, who was shot while waiting for a pizza in Hoxton, East London. After gangland members Leon Dunkley, 22, and Mohammed Smoured, 21, were jailed for 32 years for murder, it emerged that a 15-year-old boy had been hiding weapons for them. One of the guns, a Mac-10, is dubbed the "spray and pray" because it is hard to aim yet capable of firing a blistering 1,100 rounds per minute. In short, gun crime had nearly doubled in a decade, Manchester was branded Gunchester for a time, and the shadow of the gun (and knife) still hangs heavy.

Gangs

Glasgow

In February 2006, a comprehensive list of the gangs operating in Glasgow, Scotland, was published in the *Glasgow Evening Times*. The list, identified by Strathclyde Police, divided the city into north Glasgow, which had 31 gangs, south Glasgow, with 38, and east Glasgow, which boasted the highest number of gangs at 41. Gangs in Glasgow are by no means a new phenomenon – they can be traced back to the 1700s – however, with changes in society throughout history, gangs have had to reinvent themselves. Glasgow is no exception. Many of the gangland activities in the city were concentrated on fighting groups up to the 1930s, but the violence soon turned more concentrated and spawned a criminal culture which has dogged Glasgow ever since. In 1936, magistrates vowed "No Mercy for Gangsters" in the press and openly declared war on gangs. They had decided to exercise their existing powers in the courts to the fullest possible extent in a drive to wipe out gang warfare. At the time, magistrates were confident that gang suppression could not be effected by monetary penalties. Although these measures didn't completely stamp out gangs, they did have some positive effect. However, gangs remained an issue in Glasgow, and in the summer of 1968, in an attempt to stamp out gang activities, a push by the authorities was made to reduce violence in the city. In July, many of those from Glasgow's notorious gangs handed in their weapons. It resulted in one of the quietest weekends seen in the area for decades as members from four of the most dominant gangs handed in 300 weapons ranging from swords to open razors. The weapons were given up in an amnesty arranged by the singer Frankie Vaughan. The bid to end gang warfare saw, on one Saturday night, no cases of teenage violence, and the *Mirror* reported that the gangs would form a committee in mid-July and meet with Frankie Vaughan to discuss plans for a youth centre. A police spokesman at the time said: "The Glasgow Fair is a peak time for violence, but it has been quieter than usual."

On 21st July 1968, the leaders of four rival teenage gangs met with Frankie Vaughan and agreed on a "peace" treaty. They then pledged support for Frankie's £100,000 plan for a sports and social centre at Easterhouse, in the heart of Glasgow's gang warfare territory. The singer talked with the gang leaders for almost three hours at a hotel in Blackpool, where Frankie was appearing in a show. The gang leaders had been flown from Glasgow in a plane specially chartered by Frankie, and, sitting in on the talks, was the city's chief magistrate, Bailie Frank McElhone. One of the gang leaders, 17-year-old Isaac McCrae, said afterwards: "Gang warfare at Easterhouse is finished. And we speak for all the gang members." Meanwhile, it was reported that financial support for the youth centre was flooding in. However, Frankie Vaughan's good intentions did little to quash the gang warfare in Glasgow long term and gang members failed to keep their promises. From the late 1960s, street gangs and the battles between teenage thugs, territorial and mindless in their rivalry, saw a pivotal shift and it wasn't for the better. The shift involved gangs becoming involved in illegal business. Those that had made their "names" in street gangs began to turn their attention to protection rackets, working pubs, clubs and bookies, which soon, of course, led to robbery. Where there was a lethal combination of brutality and brains came yet more trouble, and it wasn't long before the likes of former street gang leaders such as Walter Norval recognized the benefits of organized crime. His gangs of armed raiders robbed hospital payrolls, wages depots and banks. His reign of terror lasted for 10 years before he was jailed (not for the first time) in 1977. The street gangs had literally matured into criminal gangs, and they took violence to a whole new level when they became interested in making money through illegal means. By the late 1970s, the street gangs turned criminal gangs once again made a shift in their organization and moved from robbery to drugs. As a result, gangs joined the underworld – they moved into a world of drug culture, underground, which took their activities out of the limelight. Policing them became a much more dangerous concept and a harder challenge for the authorities.

It was a tough time for the hard-working people of Glasgow and the police. The gangs only operated in their own areas and it was hard for police to infiltrate them. In a particularly naïve move, a number of police officers and their families were moved into some of the most deprived and dangerous areas of the city in an attempt to change the status quo of the gangs. All this led to was these families coming under frightening attacks on a daily basis.

A number of local residents did try to help the police by reporting the incidents they witnessed, but there was an acute fear of reprisals, and while the attempt did aid the force in their quest to tackle crime, as they were able to build up a picture of gang activities, it was a dangerous game. As organized crime led to money, gangs began forming affiliations with other gangs in order to distribute the drugs they were dealing. Violence was used as a means of control, but gangs were still fighting each other as a means of showing their dominance too. Many of the tenants of the former Glasgow slums were moved during the 1960s to new housing estates including Easterhouse, Drumchapel and Castlemilk. Of course, the gangs just went with them, and those who had hoped for a better life in more comfortable living conditions were sorely let down when gangs that had had to split because of the moves, just formed newer, stronger gangs. Gangs were springing up everywhere and simply followed those that had been hoping for a more peaceful existence. The issue about what to do with these new gangs, in the early 1970s, was never tackled at the highest level, and beat officers were left to cope, with little resource, as best they could. While the new housing schemes should have offered a new way of life for the decent tenants, no amenities were built and there was little feeling with regard to being part of a community. While a number of gang members were clearly just violent, others were obviously involved because there was little else to do and nowhere else to go. The media attention heaped on Glasgow's inner schemes at this time was immense and the authorities had little or no experience in how to deal with the rising issue of the gangs. Frankie Vaughan had had some success with his high-profile campaign for a weapons amnesty, and he donated money to the Easterhouse Project, but the violence continued almost unabated, apart from one "quiet" weekend in July 1968. Gang violence was horrific, calculated and callous. Those on the receiving end were scarred for life, physically and psychologically. Fear was widespread and gangs like the Tongs – operating out of Calton – had established early on that violence meant power. Working in protection rackets, the Tongs – from Tongland, as their local area was dubbed – had immense power and influence. Weapons of choice at this time included knives (the majority), swords, iron bars, hatchets, bricks and bottles.

In 2008, it was reported that Glasgow's violent crime was down by 12 per cent compared to the figures in 2007. However, Police Chief Stephen House warned that gang warfare was still prevalent in the city and required a police force dedicated to tackling violent crime. It would not be a "quick fix". The year 2008 showed a reduction across most of the violent crime categories, but police advised treating the figures with caution. They were well aware that they didn't get reports on all violent crimes committed. Many of those involved in gang warfare were reported to have stayed "silent" when approached by the authorities with regard to specific incidents. Long-term approaches to reducing knife crime, alcohol abuse and territorial violence (and crimes that had plagued the city for generations) had resulted in organizations including the Violence Reduction Unit (VRU) trying to tackle the underlying causes of gang culture. One of the issues raised was how to break the cycle of repeat offending. Other areas that the authorities tackled included domestic abuse and breaking up gangs. The following year, the buses in the Strathclyde area were dominated by hard-hitting images of what can happen to youngsters involved with a gang. The purpose was to target more than 170 gangs operating in the west of Scotland in an attempt to outline the brutal consequences of gang life. In addition, social network sites were monitored, and stop and searches were carried out routinely. Between 2008 and 2009, the VRU confiscated more than 2,750 knives and blades as part of their "Campaign Against Violence". Retailers were also targeted by police in a bid to stop the sale of knives to young people, and the public, alongside those involved in crime. They were openly encouraged to come forward about crimes they had witnessed. The fact that those living in fear of reprisals, or those who were vulnerable, did not report crimes had impacted on the effectiveness of battling gang warfare for a long time. The overall objectives with regard to gangs, in 2009, for the Strathclyde Police were to reduce the fear of crime in the local communities, remove dangerous weapons from the streets and radically hit the levels of gang violence. While the "Campaign Against Violence" was vital in the dedicated crackdown on organized crime in west Scotland, a conference held towards the end of 2012 outlined a plan that had reduced gang violence in Glasgow. The groundbreaking project involved a scheme, run in the Easterhouse area of the city – long known for its gang troubles – which led to a significant reduction in anti-social and violent crime. This 46 per cent drop in crime was hailed as a huge success and backed by Stephen House, who had recently been made chief constable of the Police Service of Scotland. Community Initiative to Reduce Violence (CIRV) had one of its largest successes in reducing territorialism. Much like the London youth charity, XLP (eXceL Project), the CIRV, which was formed in 2009, was designed to help young people make the choice not to become part of a gang. Like its London counterpart in terms of concept, the idea is that young people are offered alternatives, including youth clubs and training. They are encouraged to explore the fact that, as individuals, they have a choice not to become a gang member because, unlike in the past, there are opportunities and an alternative way of life out there for them. Targeting schools and educating youngsters in the opportunities available, as well as giving support, were cited as having helped to achieve this success. As a result, territorialism, one of the driving forces behind gang activity, has been greatly reduced in the Easterhouse area. The message to Glasgow youngsters these days is clear: "Gang activity is unacceptable." One way of tackling the problem has been to talk to final-year primary students and pupils, aged between 10 and 11, who are the most vulnerable in terms of being recruited into gangs. By showing the children in this age group other areas of life and work – rather than them having to relying on their own perceptions – it has been possible to make a difference to those who, almost ordinarily, would have become part of a gang. One of the initiatives has been to take these primary children to local fire stations. Interestingly, this has resulted in a reduction in the number of hoax calls to the service, as well as cracking down on the number of stoning attacks on the firefighters themselves. The idea of the conference to outline the scheme piloted in Easterhouse was to discuss the possibility of rolling out the project in other affected areas of Scotland. Violence has long been a big issue for Scotland and, by the end of 2012 and into the beginning of 2013, it was hoped that a number of groups would continue to work with police in order to reduce and prevent gang crimes, anti-social behaviour and organized crime, while offering alternatives through work-based schemes, youth clubs, support and understanding.

London

Glasgow wasn't the UK's only city of terror in gangland warfare. In London in 1939, about the time that Glasgow magistrates were declaring war on gangs, another flare-up of race-gang warfare threatened certain greyhound tracks and racecourses in the south of England. However, it started much earlier, in 1922, when six men were charged with shooting, with intent to murder, Fred Gilbert and George Sage in a race-gang feud. The leader of the gang charged was Joseph Sabini, who worked alongside Alfred White, George West, Simon Nyberg, Paul Bofia and Thomas Mack. Percival Clarke, prosecuting, alleged that the defendants were part of a large gang of lawless and dangerous criminals who indulged in feuds with rival gangs and who would not hesitate to use lethal weapons. On 19th August 1922, after Hurst Park races, Gilbert and Sage were outside a pub in Mornington Crescent when they were attacked by 12 men, including Sabini and his gang. The racing feud came to an end on 26th October 1922 at the Old Bailey when four of the five men eventually in the dock were convicted. Sabini and White were acquitted on the charge of intent to murder, but found guilty of shooting with intent to cause grievous bodily harm, of the unlawful possession of firearms and of riotous assembly. Nyberg was found guilty of riotous assembly only and Mack of riotous assembly and unlawfully wounding witness Amy Kent. West was found not guilty on all counts and discharged. The judge mentioned that several witnesses had been uncomfortable appearing in the box, which he felt was quite understandable when it concerned an organization such as the Bookmakers' Protection Association, where giving evidence might cause reprisals. The victims, Gilbert and Sage, along with Fred Brett, found *themselves* in court in November 1922 charged with demanding £10 with menaces from Harry Margulas. They were also accused of being in possession of firearms with intent to endanger life. The racecourse regulars had threatened the bookmaker's clerk on at least three occasions. When he sentenced the original men in November 1922, Mr Justice Roche handed out heavy sentences at the Old Bailey. Joseph Jackson received seven years penal servitude, White, five years, Sabini, three years, and George Baker, five years penal servitude. However, Sabini was admitted to the Royal Free Hospital on Gray's Inn Road in the early hours of 21st November that same year suffering from bullet wounds. He was not expected to recover. Sabini had been sitting in a club when a number of men demanded admission and made their way into the room where he was talking to his brother, "Derby" Sabini. Shots were fired from a revolver and Sabini collapsed. Four men were under arrest following the attack as police tried to trace a fifth man. Four of the men involved were said to be members of the Cortesi family – Harry Cortesi, the missing man, was said to be a bookmaker's clerk. Two men were eventually charged and convicted in 1923.

Hints of the existence of an enormous undercover "ring" controlled by a crime king in 1936, with 500 gangsters ready to carry out orders, were justified in police investigations. CID officers had discovered evidence that pointed to one man as the brains behind the gang. He was an ex-convict, convicted and sent to prison several times for crimes of violence. There was a belief that all the big London race gangs had been stamped out, but this new evidence shattered that, and additional detectives had received instructions to tear away the veil of secrecy surrounding the leader and his gang. Detectives had found that two clubs – one in the East End of London, the other in Piccadilly – were the operational hub of the gang. During the months up to November 1936, the gang leader had quietly increased the number of men in the gang and extended his various moneymaking activities.

Bookmakers had been approached with a request to buy "equipment" from the gang. If they agreed, it cost them huge sums of money. If they refused to pay then their stands were wrecked, their bags stolen and they ran the risk of ending up in hospital. Chief Inspector Sharpe of Scotland Yard, known and feared by all British racecourse criminals, was cited as planning to visit all principal meetings within 100 miles of London throughout November. Specially selected officers were to accompany him, and other plain-clothes men were detailed to move in on dog tracks. The plan was to find witnesses to the gang's fights and vendettas. It was reported that the gang leader was shielded behind a screen of bribery and terrorism. No name was released as to who the gang leader was, but gang warfare and violence continued in London in the racing world, and took a more sinister turn in the late 1940s.

"You may think it is a pity that a gang should be going out for revenge or to fight the Messina Brothers in the West End in the year 1947. If this is a plot got up by the Messinas to get the girls to give false evidence against the people in the dock, and if into that plot by mistake the police have fallen, then I think you would say the accused are not guilty." This is the summing up that Mr Justice Singleton gave the jury in April 1947, in a case in which five men claimed they were not demanding, with menaces, "protection" money from West End women of the streets, but were out to revenge a gang known as the Messina Brothers. Although the brothers were gaining notoriety on the streets of London in the aftermath of the Second World War, very few outside the capital would have heard of them before this trial. It was a saga, however, that would dominate the headlines for years to come.

The five accused – Romeo Saliba, 29, Carmcio Vassalo, 29, Paul Anthony Borg, 41, Anthony Paul Mangion, 38, and Michael Sultana, 32 – were found guilty, but Mr L Caplan, acting on behalf of Saliba, stated in his final speech that: "We say there exists in London a powerful gang of men known to the police as the Messina Brothers, who are living on the immoral earnings of women of the streets – powerful and rich, on the evidence of one of the women called who said they had two Rolls-Royces and who are able to make journeys for what purpose you may surmise to Brussels, Paris and Barcelona.

"This rich and powerful group of men is connected with the vice racket. There may be something behind and beneath the obvious facts that have come out in this case."

The accused claimed that they were out in a car in Bond Street looking for the Messinas, who, they said, had chopped off the tips of two of Vassalo's fingers. (One of the brothers, Eugene, had already been remanded on a charge at West London Magistrates Court in connection with this incident.) The accused had been informed that the Messina Brothers would be in that area that day and had driven up Bond Street demanding £1 a day "protection" money from women on the pavement. They also threatened to "carve" the women up if they did not pay.

The police found a hammer wrapped in cloth and a cosh in the car, while a later search of one of the men's flats produced a pistol and six rounds of ammunition.

Sultana was given two years for demanding money with menaces while the other four accused each received four years penal servitude. For conspiring to commit the offence, each of the five men was sentenced to two years imprisonment, to run concurrently with their other sentences.

"The evidence has satisfied me that there are in this country, and supported by this country, a great number of people who were born elsewhere and who do nothing for the support of this country," stated Mr Justice Singleton. "I am not referring to the five accused men only. I think it is desirable that attention should be drawn to the fact, in view of the difficulties of this country at the present time." While Eugene Messina was held in Wandsworth for three years for unlawfully wounding a man, his brother, Carmelo, was served a summons in October 1947, alleging that he tried to bribe a warder when visiting his brother in jail. The summons was due to be heard later that month.

Carmelo Messina "flashed" a £5 note on the visit to his brother and afterwards put it in a warder's hand, the southwest London court was told. Warder Vincent James Johnson said the brothers began to speak in a foreign language and he threatened to end the visit if they did not use English. "After that caution, I saw that Carmelo Messina was flashing what appeared to be a treasury note," he said. "I told him to put the thing away, or else he would get into trouble." At the end of the talk, Carmelo Messina touched Johnson, and he saw the man was holding a note of some sort. "I told him to put it away," Johnson added. He told the Messina gangster he didn't want the money, but was told: "Yes. You take this, sir." Messina then put the note in Johnson's right hand. Messina was accused of an alleged attempt to bribe. Questioned by Mr Casswell, KC, defending, Johnson said he took the notes because, "the man was very persistent. I thought I had evidence in my hand." Mr Casswell added that there had been some trouble at Wandsworth Prison in August 1947, where duplicated keys were being smuggled in. In November, Messina received two months for the corruption. He was also ordered to pay £50 costs. His bail was fixed at £500.

Four years later, Alfredo Messina, described as unemployed

but said to be a man of substance – he owned a £6,000 house – was charged with living on the earnings of a woman. A Scotland Yard detective said Messina had admitted knowing that the Yard had been inquiring into allegations that he and his brothers had been living for some years on the earnings of prostitutes. Messina was remanded when sureties of £400 were not paid and he was taken to Brixton Prison. When Detective Supt Guy Mahon had called on Alfredo Messina in the course of his inquiries, Messina told him he was going to give him "a lovely lunch with turkey and champagne". Later in the day a cooked turkey was found in the house and a table was laid for four. Messina was accused of living on the immoral earnings of Hermione Hindin at an address in Wembley. He pleaded not guilty and was sent for trial at the Old Bailey. Messina had tried to bribe the police with £200 at the time of their inquiries. In court, Hindin agreed that she had been convicted of prostitution but maintained that she had never given money to Messina, with whom she had lived for seven years after splitting from her husband some years before. The court was told that Mrs Hindin had 166 convictions for prostitution over 15 years, but the lady herself was unsure how many there had been. It was alleged by Messina and Hindin that the police had taken the bundles of money from their home when offered, but the couple heard them say that they would then charge Messina with bribery. In the newspapers, it was announced in May 1951 that Alfredo Messina, then aged 50, had come a long way since he played as a poor boy in the streets of Malta more than 40 years before. For the boy had big ambitions. He became as rich as he had dreamed he would. He was known to the bankers of Paris, Brussels, Casablanca and Tangier as a "wealthy dealer in diamonds". To others he was a mystery. But the fairytale lifestyle the gangster had enjoyed came to an end when he was convicted at the Old Bailey and his dark secrets caught up with him. He was jailed for two years for living on the immoral earnings of Hindin, and for the corruption. His conviction marked the beginning of an all-out drive by Scotland Yard in London's West End "square mile" of vice. For the Home Office – following plans by the bishop of London and by deputations of prominent men from London boroughs – had set up an official committee to examine the problems. Alfredo Messina, immaculately groomed in a stylishly cut suit with a silk breast-pocket handkerchief clipped with a silver pencil, left the dock for prison with the judge's words in his ears: "You thought so far as the police of this country were concerned money could do anything. You are an evil man." Messina was fined £500 on the charge of corruption. Messina had arrived in London in 1939 when he fled from Brussels at the outbreak of the Second World War. He brought with him a fortune of £30,000. Though within the age limits for national service, he did not serve in the Forces, or do any work of national importance. He stated he suffered from high blood pressure and diabetes. He was known to mix with a curious set in Mayfair – but only during the months in 1951 had Scotland Yard managed to get proof of his life and his crimes. They learned that he had been seen in his car many evenings taking a convicted prostitute to the streets of the West End, and returning in the early hours to take her back to Wembley. Messina told the court the only income tax returns he had made were in connection with his house. He alleged that Mahon and his deputy, Foster, had wrongly accused him of offering the bribe. Here was a man who had built up a fortune from vice. Next in the press was Attilio Messina, 41, who refused to have his fingerprints taken. He was remanded in custody in November 1951, charged with procuring a woman in 1945 to become a prostitute and living on her earnings in 1945, 1946 and 1947. He was sent to jail that same month for six months for his crimes. The Crown, it was stated, had decided not to proceed on two other charges of procuring the prostitute or living on her earnings in other years. A solicitor for Eugene Messina was then suspended for three years by the Law Society in July 1953, due to references being "unjustified" when supplied by him to estate agents on behalf of his brother and Mrs Hindin. William Perey Webb, of Grays Inn, London, had acted for Eugene Messina since 1948, and in 1950 Webb's firm informed an estate agent that Messina would prove "a responsible tenant", even though the solicitor knew the brother had been in Wandsworth Prison. The clerk acting on behalf of Webb, Watson, also signed a letter stating that Mrs Hindin was a "respectable and responsible person".

In April 1956 two Belgian women, who were key prosecution witnesses in the Messina brothers' "white slavery" trial, disappeared. They had made written statements to the police several weeks before, but then they vanished and it was thought that they had left the country. The trial was due to open on 29th April. The Messina brothers – Eugene and Carmelo, both considered "Vice Kings of Soho" – were charged with procuring white women. They were also accused of carrying firearms, possessing false passports and illegally entering Belgium. They were arrested in a fashionable bar at the Belgian coastal resort of Knokke in August 1955. The notorious brothers had fled from Britain four years earlier, and were alleged to have directed a network of international vice from a sumptuous, 10-roomed flat in the select Avenue Louise in Brussels. Police said that they were still controlling Soho vice dens from across the Channel. The parents of the missing Belgian girls arrived in court in Bruges in May 1956. But their daughters, Elizabeth de Meester, 22, and Marie Vervaecke, 24, did not appear. It was believed that the two young women were still in Britain. The judge agreed to the plea of the Messina brothers that the charges against them should be heard in French, and transferred the trial to Tournai – a French-speaking town in southern Belgium. The case was due to take place within two months. The brothers were charged with procuring and attempting to procure women, having entered Belgium illegally on false passports, and possessing firearms.

Meanwhile, back in London a month later, MPs in the Commons demanded that gangs and the vice trade in London – which was "shocking" – should be "cleaned up". The home secretary,

Major Lloyd George, was asked how long the public would have to wait before the activities of these "squalid, cowardly, small-time hoodlums" were effectively crushed. The home secretary was also asked if he felt that the police were taking "effective" steps against the criminal fraternity. He replied that he was "satisfied" the police were giving "close and urgent attention" to the prevention of crimes of violence. Labour MP Anthony Greenwood retorted that although the home secretary might be satisfied, there was "mounting public disquiet". After referring to razor-slashing in the West End, Greenwood said that in three recent cases at the Old Bailey there had been blatant perjury. Judges had had to be provided with police escorts and gangs of 12 or more paraded up and down outside the court while cases were being heard. Mr Justice Donovan, who had jailed two West End gangsters for seven years each for a brutal attack, told the jury: "It sounds like Chicago in the worst days of prohibition rather than London in 1956." Lloyd George said that while the two men jailed for the attack on Jack Spot and their gangs were known to police, it was not possible to "just round them up like taking stray dogs to Battersea". Another MP said that the danger of "this ugly situation" was that of the public losing confidence in the police. "Is it not a fact that if really drastic instructions were given from the top the whole of this filthy business could be cleared up in a few weeks?" asked Lieutenant-Colonel Lipton, a Labour MP from Brixton. Lloyd George felt that the public were not losing their faith in the police and he said: "You get cycles of these outbreaks and it is an extremely difficult thing, because most of these chaps are known to the police. But it is difficult to prevent the crime simply because you know the man is a criminal." The discussion then turned to two girls who had paid £5,000 each a year to the Messina brothers, and the suspicion that properties they had bought in London in Curzon Street, Chesterfield Terrace, Stafford Street in Mayfair and Shepherd Market were being used as brothels. Another MP produced a list of names of 22 girls who had paid immoral earnings to the Messina brothers. While Lloyd George did not appear to worry about the newspaper criticisms of himself, he felt that critics of the police had been "grossly" unfair.

Police forces in France, the UK, Belgium and Italy had all been working together to compile evidence against the Messinas. It was revealed that a number of women working for the brothers had been asked to give evidence against them, but all had refused. Sergeant Gentle and Inspector Margaret Heald were both in Belgium for the trial. They heard strong criticism of Scotland Yard by defence lawyers appearing for the Messina brothers. One lawyer said: "If prostitution is so rife, why haven't police taken drastic measures to stamp it out? And, why didn't they get a conviction against the Messinas when they prosecuted them for living on immoral earnings?

"The London police not only failed to convict the Messina brothers, but send people over here who know practically nothing about them. Do we have to take what they say as evidence?"

Sergeant Gentle said: "I know a large number of the Messina

girls, about 20 altogether. I know that the Messina brothers – five of them – have criminal records.

"They own various premises in London, which are used for prostitution. They all have a lot of money. One of the brothers, Alfredo, has served two years imprisonment for living on immoral earnings."

Inspector Heald told the court that some French and Belgian girls married Britons to get to London and then separated from them almost immediately. She had investigated some of the "marriages of convenience", and one of the girls interviewed was Marie Vervaecke, who had married George Smith, an ex-policeman who had needed the money. The court was told how one girl earned £2,490 in six weeks, working as a prostitute for the Messinas. Sitting in court, listening, were Eugene and Carmelo, who were both flanked by armed officers. The public prosecutor, Jean de Bettenbourg, opening the case, said the police had found documents showing that the Messinas "were engaged in white slavery". He said the two brothers were known to the "police of the whole world". Commissioner Anton Cuppens, of the Belgian CID, told the court that Eugene Messina owned four properties in London which were believed to be brothels. He said that land certificates for the buildings were found in a safe deposit box in the Bank of Brussels after the brothers' arrest. The safe deposit was in the name of Augustine Veriet, or Johans, "a convicted prostitute and Messina madam". It was also revealed that it was thought that the brothers were Red spies. They had been caught out for being too greedy, when trying to import girls from Eastern Germany into the UK. Counter-intelligence agents got on to the brothers' track when telephone operators in Brussels reported frequent calls from the sumptuous flat occupied by them to women in East Berlin. Agents tapped the lines, decided that it was nothing to do with espionage and passed their findings to CID in Belgian. It led to the vice trail that now saw them in court. MPs in London then demanded more answers and a more effective solution to the vice problems in the city. Meanwhile, a girl charged in July 1956 with soliciting was not told to pay the usual maximum fine. Instead, the magistrates ordered her to find a surety of £25 for her "good behaviour" for 12 months, or face 12 months in jail. The woman, Brenda Hill, 19, from Paddington, London, was arrested in Hyde Park at 2.30 in the afternoon, while five other women – also arrested for soliciting (although they were all picked up after dark) – were all charged the maximum fine of £2. It was also suggested – in London – that men involved in sex offences should be punished just as much as the women were. As the law stood at the time, it was possible for the vice traffic to be carried on without anyone being able to bring the real culprits to book. The fining of the women was a farce, according to former home secretary, Chuter Ede. In dealing with prostitution, the police were still using powers under acts as old as the Vagrancy Act of 1824. On 6th July 1956, Carmelo Messina drank iced lager at a roadside café in a Belgian town, while a mile away Convict No. A140823 – his brother Eugene – had started a seven-year sentence for white slavery, and faced his first meal, of boiled cod and watery cabbage, in his new prison surroundings. The evidence given in the trial by Scotland Yard is what had convicted Eugene. Carmelo had been sentenced to 10 months in jail for illegal entry into Belgium on a false passport and possessing firearms, but his time in prison between August and the following July saw his immediate release. However, he was looking for a new home. The authorities had ordered him out of Belgium within 48 hours. Two days later, Carmelo simply disappeared and police were warned to "arrest him on sight". The 24-hour "safe-conduct" pass he had been issued had expired, and he was now wanted as an "undesirable alien". He had hoped to apply for a British passport and return to the UK, but he had failed to do this. He had been driven from Tournai to Brussels in a hired car before he vanished. Police were convinced that he was still in Belgium, where he was not wanted. Meanwhile, while the Belgians considered Messina to be British, the British authorities regarded the man as Italian. Later, in July, police lodged appeals for a review of the sentences passed on the Messina brothers in Tournai, saying they were too lenient. In a twist, in December 1956 Eugene's sentence was cut by seven months by the Brussels Appeal Court, while Carmelo's was increased by two months and he received another year for an attempt to procure a white girl. He was, however, still on the run.

A few months earlier, in June 1956, Scarface Jack (Spot) Comer was escorted by police from the Old Bailey after the two men he swore *did not* attack him were each jailed for seven years.

Comer sat beside his wife, Rita, who had identified the men, as the two were driven from the court after hearing the judge's sentencing. The sentences were signalled to Billy Hill, a known gangster, outside the Old Bailey, as he stood waiting in a crowd. Rita Comer had also identified Billy as one of her husband's attackers, but police had agreed during the trial there wasn't enough evidence to support this. Billy Hill had waited outside the court since the morning of 15th June 1956 alongside at least 10 other men. In-between sipping cups of tea in a café, Hill spent his time sitting in a seat marked "Remembrance" in a churchyard nearby. Hill and his followers left after hearing the result of the case. He had gone by the time Comer and his wife were driven away by police. During the dramatic trial of Fraser and Warren, Comer had heard himself described as "the King of the Underworld, the scum of the earth". It was feared that the court case against Fraser and Warren would see the flare-up of gang warfare. Police vehicles were on standby and Scotland Yard was aware of the ongoing power struggle between bosses of the underworld in the racing fraternity. In his defence of Robert Warren, counsel Patrick Marrinan had described Comer as a: "Vile, cut-throat gangster ... that corner boy of the lowest ilk." Comer (and his wife, who was struck on the head) had been attacked by four men who had raced towards them. The case had a background which was "unnatural". It showed, according to press reports, that people were "prepared to go to the most tremendous lengths to pay off feuds". Comer hadn't wanted the case, stating that it had nothing to do with the police and was his "business"; however, the authorities were not prepared to let the attack remain underground when gangs were running riot in the West End of London with knives and committing "grave" assaults.

Success, it was deemed, went to the strongest gang members, or those with the sharpest knives. Comer, a bookmaker, was cited as having said that he was "cleaning up" in the racing world, where gangs were intimidating bookmakers. The case, it appeared, was centred on race-gang warfare. Warren had already had five previous convictions, but none were for violence. They related to dishonesty or contravention of the betting laws while carrying out his job as an assistant to bookmakers. Frankie Fraser, on the other hand, had 15 previous convictions for dishonesty, robbery and violence. In January 1951, he had been sentenced at Clerkenwell, London, to six months in prison for assault, and in February that year was sentenced to three months for malicious damage. In 1948, while serving a prison sentence, he was certified insane and removed to a mental hospital. He was discharged in 1949, seemingly recovered. In 1952 he was sentenced to three years imprisonment, and was again certified insane during his time in prison. He was transferred to Broadmoor and discharged in 1955. Frankie Fraser had taken to a life of crime at the age of 14, on the fringe of Soho, by becoming a gang member.

Just a few days later, following the Spot case in 1956, there was a debate in the House of Lords with regard to race-gang warfare, and it was cited that a clean-up in the betting laws was a prerequisite for a strike at the razor gangs. Lord Pakenham, a Labour peer, said: "If we do nothing now in the two Houses of Parliament and allow things to drift, then the responsibility will fall on our shoulders if the worst evils of Chicago are produced and sustained in the heart of London." He was supporting a motion by Tory peer Viscount Astor, welcoming the Government's intention to bring in a Bill to reform the betting laws. Lord Pakenham said there was no single reason more responsible for what was going on in the underworld than the present laws on betting. "Owing to the great temptations offered, there seems to exist a situation in certain sections of the Metropolitan Police which must cause great anxiety," he declared.

Viscount Astor, a breeder and owner of racehorses, said that the betting laws were unanimously condemned by the Royal Commission on Betting, which had reported five years before on the situation. They were difficult to enforce, out of date, full of class distinctions, and led to an alliance between bookmakers and criminals. What it was thought was needed was a law which could be enforced, was fair to all, and did not offer temptation for dishonesty in the sport. It was mooted that British racing could be transformed if a further £3 million was injected into the sport for the right reasons. Lord Astor said: "Perhaps if we had had all these Jack Spot and other troubles at the time the Commission sat, they might have taken the view that the Tote monopoly would have been a fine thing." He went on to say that he hoped the Government would at least accept the recommendation of the Royal Commission that all bookmakers should be licensed and supervised. He then explained there was "a sinister alliance" between the Committee of the Churches on Betting and the bookmakers to oppose betting shops. The Churches Committee thought that to have betting shops would encourage betting and make it too respectable. "The alternative to the legalized betting office is the street bookie, illegal as at present and tending to corrupt the police and going into gang warfare," Lord Astor continued. The bishop of Sheffield, Dr L S Hunter, said the Church was convinced the present betting system produced certain "evils". It was, he said, in the public interest to have a Bill before Parliament as quickly as possible. Lord Mancroft, under-secretary at the Home Office, recalled the Government's promise to bring in a Bill setting up betting shops and bringing the betting laws up to date. Many experts and about 20 different bodies had been consulted by 1956, while Scotland Yard revealed in July that year that five detectives had successfully infiltrated the London "underworld". For eight months, the detectives had disguised themselves as mobsters – wearing "flashy" clothes and living the lives of race-gang members. Tough, experienced officers were chosen for the "Ghost Squad" as it was known.

One detective adopted his "double life" so successfully that it was understood he had been accepted as a regular member of a race gang. Each detective gave firsthand information about the haunts and activities of many razor-wielding gang members. Scotland Yard had produced a report that dealt with more than a score of Soho and East End characters about whom Yard chiefs were anxious to know more. The head of the Yard's detectives, Assistant Commissioner Jackson, called a meeting of senior officers to discuss the report: it was believed to have been one of the most decisive meetings ever held at Scotland Yard. One immediate remit was that Jackson ordered the increase in inquiries in Soho and the West End as a result of the Jack Spot case. The signal for an intensified campaign against mobsters was sent to all stations under the command of the head of the Soho and West End districts, Chief Superintendent Ted Greene. The then home secretary, Major Lloyd George, was informed of the proposed new police action to "clean up" London.

Carmelo Messina was finally jailed in November 1958 after landing in the United Kingdom without the permission of the immigration authorities and failing to produce a passport. He was given six months. The judge who sentenced him said that there would be a recommendation to deport him. "So far as the law is concerned, this man is an alien," said Sir Gerald Dodson, Recorder of London at the Old Bailey.

By 1959 gangs were on the increase, and 18-year-old Alan Johnson was murdered in Barking, Essex, at a rock 'n' roll dance for telling the truth about where he came from. He was stabbed to death in the back, stomach and heart for answering a gang of youths who asked him where he came from. When he responded that he was from Canning Town, he was immediately attacked. In an ironic twist, Alan Johnson died to the strains of Elvis Presley's *Don't Be Cruel*. His death marked the climax of a period of teenage gang warfare centred on rock 'n' roll dance halls in Barking, Romford and Dagenham. Police believe that the fight during which Alan was murdered was "in return" for an attack on a youth at a Romford dance hall three weeks earlier. However, it was not thought that Alan Johnson had anything to do with the Romford incident: he simply came from the wrong area. One of the organizers of the event where Alan died, Tom Singleton, 22, said: "The trouble started about 20 minutes before the end. One of my bouncers moved in to stop the fight. I told my other six bouncers to go and help. But, someone overheard me and told the bouncers, 'If you go in there, you'll be done up, too.' Outside in the street, I saw another crowd waiting for trouble. Then I heard the girls inside starting to scream. Someone was carried into the office. I followed and saw Alan Johnson lying on the floor in a pool of blood. The fight didn't finish there. It carried on in the street outside. Then everyone vanished like magic."

Also in 1959, in February, Attilio Messina was back in court where it was alleged that he had received £40,000 from one woman's earnings as a prostitute. The allegation was made at Marlborough Street Court, London, when Messina was charged with – between 1947 and February 1959 – procuring a woman named Edna Kaliman to become a prostitute. A second charge alleged that Messina, on certain dates, had lived wholly or in part on the earnings of prostitution. A third charge was similar. Messina, an antique dealer living in Hammersmith, was accused in the name of Raymond Maynard, but a police witness referred to him as Attilio Messina. The police witness, Detective Chief Inspector John du Rose, told the magistrates that, with another officer, he saw Messina in King Street, Hammersmith, and confronted him. Messina was cautioned and charged and taken to West End Central police station. Messina insisted he had been framed. However, Mayfair prostitute Edna Kaliman told the court in March 1959 that she had earned £40,000 in eight years and handed it all to Attilio Messina. She kept nothing for herself, she added, and during her association with Messina "there were always threats". Kaliman was giving evidence at Marlborough Street Court, where the 48-year-old Messina brother was accused. Oliver Nugent, prosecuting, said that Mrs Kaliman, who was separated from her husband, would tell "the story of a prostitute". She said she met Messina in 1947, when he offered her a lift as she was on her way home. Later she stayed the night with Messina in the Kensington flat to which he took her. After further "dates", covering 18 months, Mrs Kaliman continued: "He offered me a flat in Knightsbridge ... I accepted the offer." Mrs Kaliman went on: "The flat was not in my name. Later I found out it was in the name of another girl who was with him." When Nugent asked if Messina imposed any conditions on what she was to do when she got the flat, Mrs Kaliman said: "I went there at the end of May, 1949, and I was not allowed to go out until about the August. He provided the food." Asked if Messina eventually put a proposition to her, Mrs Kaliman replied: "Yes, he said I could make some easy money. He knew someone who would train me to do this. I was then introduced to a woman who took me to a flat in Shepherd Market." Oliver Nugent said: "What were you to do for this easy money?" Mrs Kaliman said: "When I went to Shepherd Market the woman called me in for clients …" "You had to become a prostitute?" said Nugent. "Yes," said Kaliman. Mrs Kaliman said Messina told her this life would be for 18 months to two years – then they were to have a life together. Asked how Messina treated her, Mrs Kaliman said that when she was in the flat in Knightsbridge she had a "good hiding" when some furniture was brought and she did not sign the receipt. After a week in Shepherd Market, Mrs Kaliman confirmed she was given a flat in King's Yard, Davies Street, in Mayfair. She was taken there by Messina and introduced to a maid. She said her "instructions" were to work through Maddox Street, George Street, Brook Street and the part of Bond Street that ran to Maddox Street. She did not know how much she earned but it was in the region of £120 to £140 per week. She kept no money for herself, but paid the maid and then handed the rest to Messina. Later she went to a top flat in Bond Street. "That flat was in the name of Charles Maitland. His other name was Carmelo Messina. I was in Bond Street for eight years until February this year. All that time I was earning money by prostitution – about £40,000. It was all handed over to the accused."

Asked why this went on so long, Mrs Kaliman replied: "I was absolutely terrified. There were always threats – that he would put me out in the street in my slippers and reduce me to nothing. He threatened that if I ever had any ideas of getting away from him he would cut my face. I had one or two nasty blows on my jaw."

The case continued. Two more women came forward. A chance meeting at a phone box ... a chance meeting at a bus stop. The two women told the court that this was how Attilio Messina had come into their lives. The women gave evidence at Clerkenwell in London, where Messina was standing trial. Both the women who gave evidence wrote down their names and addresses in court, rather than have them publically announced. The phone box meeting was in Knightsbridge in 1952 said Woman No. 1. She allowed the man – Messina – to use the box first and afterwards he offered her a lift. He later took her out to dinner. Subsequently, she stayed with him on several occasions at a flat he had in Morden, Surrey. She knew Messina as Maynard. He told her she could better herself and said he would give her a job in a sweet shop. Eventually she left her parents' home and went to live with him in Morden. The woman then told the court that on one occasion Maynard asked her to go to a wardrobe and get out a briefcase. "He took out a long buff envelope and it had 'Will of Attilio Messina' written on it," she said. Messina then asked her if it meant anything to her and she replied no. He then said she must be "greener" than he thought. She lived at Morden for three or four months and eventually he said he would like to introduce her to "a very good friend" whose name was Edna. Asked if Messina gave any reason for wanting to introduce her to Edna the woman replied that he indicated that "she would introduce me to very rich clients". The woman said that she met Edna and went with her to a West End flat, where she stayed for about a week. She confirmed that here she had had to "help with the proceedings". The woman agreed with Oliver Nugent that the "proceedings" were, in fact, prostitution. She said she got £4 that week, which she gave to "Maynard". The woman said she left the flat because she became frightened and did not want to do "those things".

The bus stop meeting was described by Woman No. 2, who had met Messina in 1943 or 1944. She had been waiting with a girlfriend at the bus stop when the man she knew as "Maynard" came along in a car and offered them a lift, which they accepted. There were intervals of years in their subsequent meetings, and then, in 1953, she stayed with Maynard at Morden for a couple of days. Afterwards, he introduced her to Edna. She was told to stay at the flat that Edna lived in until she "knew how to go about things". The woman said she stayed at the flat only a few days. Edna was very kind and treated her well, she added. Mrs Kaliman's former maid was next in court and told of events in the two flats. She also knew Messina as Mr Maynard and referred to him as "the Boss". She also wrote down her name and address in court before giving evidence. She said she had started work for Mrs Kaliman in 1949, and it was later that year that she first met Messina. This was at a flat in King's Yard, where she was employed as maid for Edna, who was working as a prostitute. It was the maid's job to collect the money and, at the end of the evening, hand it to Edna. The amount varied she said, but it was anywhere between £10 and £30 each night. They remained in the flat for a short time before being moved to Bond Street where things carried on exactly as they had done up to this point. While in the company of Edna and Messina the maid said that nothing untoward had happened to her employer, but she said she was well aware that Messina did beat Mrs Kaliman. Asked if she had anything special to do when clients called, the maid told the court that if a client stayed more than 10 minutes, she was required to knock on the door. She added: "I was reprimanded by the Boss once because I was told I was not helping her [Edna] enough." The ex-maid added: "One night in the car he asked me why Edna was not pulling her weight. He did not think she was making enough money. I said she was ill and needed a holiday." Messina then called a doctor to Mrs Kaliman and she had remained in bed for about a week. In one year, there were three other girls in the flat. But they only stayed a short time, said the maid. The maid then admitted that she had done everything she could to persuade the girls not to stay. She also then told the court that she had walked out of the flat four years before the trial.

Messina tried twice, in vain, to get bail, and pleaded not guilty to the charges against him. Scotland Yard detective, Sergeant Denis Welsh, told the *London Recorder*: "There is no doubt that if given the opportunity, Messina will intimidate prosecution witnesses. The main witness in this case has, in fact, disclosed that should Messina be at large, she herself will go missing, and we will have great difficulty putting her before the court."

Meanwhile, Attilio's brother, Carmelo, who had served his time in Wandsworth Prison, was told he would be deported, by the Home Office, to Rome. Carmelo Messina was deported from Britain on 22nd March 1959. He was met in Rome by Italian police. They then took him to an airport office and questioned him for four hours. He was driven to the police headquarters in Rome following the questioning and was held. Police were still undecided about what to do with him. It was mooted that he might be expelled to a small village in Sicily, Linguaglossa. Messina was eventually transported to the village, but he took one look and tried to return to Rome. He was stopped at Rome airport by detectives. He was told he must stay in the village, chosen because the Messina family originated from there. Attilio Messina was jailed for four years the following month for having kept Edna Kaliman "enslaved" for 10 years. Newspaper reports revealed that Mrs Kaliman had been given £7 per week for her hairdresser, telephone and food, but she had been forced to work on any day of the week, whether she was well or ill. Messina eventually pleaded guilty to procuring Mrs Kaliman to become a prostitute. The story of her "slavery" was told by Mervyn Griffith-Jones, prosecuting. Over the time that the former dressmaker was enslaved, due to the stress and her deteriorating health,

Edna's earnings fell from around £130 a week to £50. Her letters from her parents were censored and she lived under the constant threats with which Messina controlled her. A doctor advised Mrs Kaliman to have a month's rest. As she and Messina left the surgery, he told her that was "rubbish" and she should "work on". After trouble with Messina over a police visit to another prostitute at the same address, Edna Kaliman decided to "get away from it all". She went home to her mother, who lived in Derbyshire, and told her story. Then she went to the police.

In 1959, the five "evil" Messina brothers were "smashed". The vice kings had brought the level of organized crime and vice in London to heights previously only seen in Chicago. They used Chicago methods in order to maintain their control over those they associated with and to generate fear. The five brothers were Attilio, Carmelo, Alfredo, Eugene and Salvatore. In the beginning the brothers imported girls from across the European continent, and their methods were always the same. They posed as wealthy businessmen and spoke sincerely of marriage. Under this promise, seduction followed and then moral degradation. The girls could not go back to their families. The next move was to put the girls under the tutelage of a seasoned prostitute. Often a girl would go through a "marriage of convenience" to a stranger to give her his name and nationality – the cost of which was £10. Then the vice-peddling brothers would install the girl in a luxury flat and give her a "beat" in Mayfair, which consisted of around 20 yards of pavement. With the flat went a maid to keep check on the number of customers, and a man, known as a "ponce", to watch the Messina interests. All the money earned by the girls had to be paid to the brothers. The girls, in return, were housed, clothed, fed and given pocket money. One girl got one day off in a year, and that was only when her parents came to visit from Belgium. They thought their daughter worked in export. The Messina brothers prospered for a long time. The girls – there were more than 100 of them at any one time – were too scared to talk. Police who tried to smash the brothers were hindered by the difficulties of enforcing the vice laws and because the brothers knew how to evade them. Each of them apparently had a genuine business, so it was difficult to prove they were living on the immoral earnings of the prostitutes. Their incomes were fabulous – and so were their flats, their cars and their clothes. Eugene had a Rolls-Royce. They all went to the best tailors. Their shirts were silk, handmade and monogrammed. They paid women who had grown old in prostitution to watch the younger ones and to collect the money. The same women brought recruits to the filthy business. Once any girl who was in the brothers' clutches tried to get away, she was threatened with a "cutting". Some who tried were marked for life ... and even then were still so frightened that they would not identify their attackers, but by the middle of 1959 – with Eugene and Attilio in prison and Carmelo deported – the brothers' reign of terror had come to an end. A moving appeal against branding these girls as "common prostitutes" for life was held in the Commons in April

1959. Leslie Hale, Labour MP for West Oldham, urged that no girl under the age of 18 should be convicted of soliciting. The Street Offences Bill – aimed at cleaning up the streets of London and other big cities – provided for fines of up to £25 and jail sentences of up to three months for prostitutes who persistently solicited in the streets. Speaking with great emotion, Hale said that if the Home Office really tried, they could find thousands of decent families in London who would give homes to girls under 18 who had gone astray. Once a girl was convicted and branded as a prostitute it was much more difficult to persuade her to live a better life, he claimed. "At this moment, there are girls of 16 and 17, hawking their bodies in Hyde Park," said Hale. "Most of them are organized, either by men of the Messina type or by older women." Hale's proposal was defeated by a Government majority of 73, and the Bill was finally approved by 131 votes to 25. It was expected to go to the House of Lords and be passed as law in 1959. Meanwhile, later that year, Eugene Messina was released early for "good conduct". He was escorted to the French border by Belgium police after his release and was believed to have set up home, living in great luxury, on the French Riviera. It was a very different story for youngest brother, Carmelo, who died of a brain haemorrhage in a seedy Sicilian boarding house. He had made a six-figure fortune, but ended his life in squalor in a ramshackle room.

Two years later, in September 1961, Justice Lawton gave a warning as he jailed eight London gangsters: "Gunmen cannot be tolerated and will not be tolerated in the streets of London. The law of England has no use for them."

The eight men, members of rival East End gangs, had fought with choppers, a kukri (curved Indian knife) and shotguns after a quarrel at a Canning Town wedding. All eight stood together in the dock at the Old Bailey. Before passing sentences ranging up to three years, the judge said: "A great boast in this city of ours is that it is law abiding. All of you have disgraced it by carrying on gang warfare of a very serious kind. It is the kind of conduct for which judges of this country can find no mercy." The eight men were all found guilty of unlawful assembly. They included, from the Canning Town Gang, James Daly, 23, Derek Whincup, 26, and Herbert Summer, 28, all of Malmesbury Road, Canning Town, and, from the Custom House Gang, Maurice Nichol, 21, of Shipman Road, Custom House, Albert Reading, 29, of Bradley Street, Canning Town, Robert Reading, 21, of Chauntler Road, Custom House, Joseph Reading, 35, of Clinch Court, Canning Town and Terence Emberson, 22, of Barnes Court, Custom House. Albert and Robert Reading, Nichol, Daly, Summer and Whincup were also found guilty of being in unlawful possession of offensive weapons, and Daly, Summer and Whincup were convicted of being in possession of a firearm with intent to endanger life. Daly, Summer and Whincup were each jailed for three years; Albert Reading and Nichol were jailed for two and a half years; Robert Reading got 18 months; Joseph Reading got nine months.

London's Little Italy, EC1, saw the blood flow in October 1962 when this forgotten part of the capital, a half-square mile of the Italian colony, saw the death of Mary O'Donnell. She was found battered to death in her Clerkenwell Road shop. The devout Roman Catholic sold plaster Madonnas, prayer books and other religious objects. Little Italy had emerged more than 100 years earlier when Italian immigrants centred their community around St Peter's Italian Church, in a little maze of streets that had long since been bulldozed to make way for a car park. The Italian community had brought with them the customs of southern Italy. They made barrel organs, worked the streets as knife-grinders and sold hokey-pokey ice cream. With these immigrants came the gangsters. The decent Italians, English, Irish and French who settled in the area were peaceful law-abiding citizens who lived in tumbledown houses and council flats (where tin baths still hung from the walls). However, in the early 1960s, many of the Italians had moved away. The death of Mary O'Donnell was only the second death in Little Italy, despite the lawless years between the First and Second World Wars when, in other tough quarters of London, barely a weekend passed without violence. The first killing in Little Italy came in 1925, when a stabbing took place. It was gang related. Little Italy was renowned for being friendly, but it also attracted the less desirable. In 1925 the Sabini gang was fighting to control the racecourses (the family lived in Little Italy). It was the same year that the Birmingham Race Gang came down to London to fight the Sabini gang. Gambling took place in the streets on a regular basis and people bet for pennies. There is little to suggest what happened to Mary O'Donnell, but she obviously wasn't part of a gang.

In January 1964, Scotland Yard feared new gang wars. The threat of gang warfare hung over London's betting shops after the shooting of former boxer, 33-year-old Ted Berry. Berry, a British ex-boxing hopeful known as the "Keg of Dynamite", was a £15-a-week betting-shop clerk. He was shot as he walked down the street near his East End home at Hadrian Estate, Hackney Road, Bethnal Green. The shot came from a car. Then, as he lay on the pavement writhing in agony, witnesses saw a man leap from a car and shoot Berry again – through the left leg. The gunman jumped back into the car and escaped. On 12th January 1964, it was reported that the victim was "progressing" in hospital after having his left leg amputated, while his family gathered at the council flat he shared with his wife and three children for a meeting. His father, boxing trainer Harry "Kid" Berry, said: "The phone has been going all weekend with people ringing up asking what they can do to help to find the men who shot Teddy." He was understandably worried that someone would decide to take the law into their own hands in order to avenge the attack. The victim's wife, Joyce Berry, 35, comforted her three children and said: "Ted was very popular with everyone in this area. All his friends are on the lookout to find who shot him." Berry's brother, a boxer known as "Checker", said: "Teddy was in the pub drinking with me and went home, about 200 yards, to get his tobacco tin. He was shot on the way back to the pub.

"The second shot was aimed deliberately to maim him, fired about eight inches from his knee. It was done with a double-barrelled shotgun using pellets." Scotland Yard, hunting the gunman and the man who drove the car, feared that gang warfare would break out. For some time, they had known that trouble was brewing between rival gangs in the East End. The trouble began in August 1963, when a petrol bomb was thrown into a betting shop. Later, two more petrol bombs partially destroyed other betting shops. Three gangs were known to be operating in the East End through protection rackets. They had been targeting betting shops that had been making good money. If the shops fail to pay, then violent action was inevitable. Berry, who had retired from amateur boxing after he lost an eye in the ring, worked for a betting shop in Green Dragon Yard, off Commercial Street. Detectives sat by his hospital bed hoping that he could help them identify his attacker.

By 1968, things were no better in the capital and a spotlight was shone on the rising cost of defying the underworld. On 13th February that year, a *Mirror* article by Tom Tullett highlighted that: "Once again the guns are blazing in London. And once again innocent people are terrified." They were scared, not only by the guns, but also by the word "aggravation". The whole situation was striking fear into people whose only aim was a quiet life – like most of the people who lived in Hazlebury Road, Fulham, who witnessed gangland murder in their midst. A shooting in

Hazlebury Road involved a bullet in the chest for Terence Elgar, although none of the witnesses would admit to having heard a thing. Quite simply, they were too scared to talk. One man said it would "aggravate them if I told you". Aggravate was the word of the moment. Anyone said to be "aggravating" was either beaten up or shot. "There was a time when fists, clubs or razors were used to settle scores when the big gangs fell out," wrote Tullett. "Gradually, the gun came into fashion, the object being to maim. But recently even that penalty has been stepped up. 'Aggravation' now carries the threat of sudden death by carefully planned ambush. In the last three years, gun crimes have trebled and it is certain that as many guns are used in gang vendettas as the payroll raids," he continued. London hospitals had long lists of men who had been shot, many of whom had suffered amputation. Yet none of the men had been able to identify their assailants. Most victims found it better to stay quiet, because if they talked they risked the chance of another bullet. If they remained quiet, they might be allowed to live in peace, or even be paid for their silence.

There were others, however, who reacted more aggressively, by setting up armed mobs of their own for reprisals. So, the gang wars escalated. At the time Tullett was writing, it was believed that the vendettas were all down to London's scrap metal business. However, five years later, Tom Tullett was writing that "police are on the winning side at last". In the *Mirror* on 5th September 1973, he claimed that "ruthless mobsters of the East

End underworld are badly frightened men". He wrote that these men were "also men with a chip on their shoulder. A chip so large, detectives believe that the bomb which blew up three policemen at West Ham … was deliberately planted by a gang seeking to avenge the big police purge." The purge had steadily been gaining in momentum over the previous six years. However, in the 18 months to September 1973, it had been hotting up quite considerably. During this time, more than 80 gang members had been arrested and charged with serious robberies. More than 30 gang members had been charged with using intimidation to get money from businesses, and new gangs trying to take over where the Krays left off had been either wiped out or stopped from spreading. The big police crackdown had given the East End – acknowledged cradle of the underworld – one shock after another, according to Tullett. It was known that police really did think they had clamped down on gangland activities after the Krays found themselves in prison in 1969, but, as we know now, the Krays were still "hard at work" keeping the Firm going from their cells by acting as consultants and lending the family name to those willing and able to pay for it.

However, in 1973 the police were celebrating their triumph at the crackdown the "purge" had seemed to bring about. The most ecstatic about results at the time was the Serious Crime Squad, led by Detective Chief Superintendent Albert Wickstead, while newspapers implied that gangland was "on the run", and also stated that gangs were "struggling for survival". Of course, today, we know just how well they did manage to survive and the legacy that led to a new era of gang warfare.

Returning to the crackdown by police following the imprisonment of the Krays, 12 men were arrested by Scotland Yard's "gang-buster" squad after a series of dawn swoops in April 1972. Eleven of the men were accused of offences including attempted murder, causing grievous bodily harm and illegal possession of firearms. The 12th man was charged with receiving stolen property. Three of the men were from the same family. One of them was 25-year-old professional boxer Jimmy Tibbs, whose charges included three attempted murders. All 12 appeared at Old Street Court in London on 6th April 1972. The dawn raids had been carried out the week before, and 20 men were arrested. All were taken to City Road police station in London's East End and were questioned for many hours by Wickstead. Tibbs was accused of attempting to murder Terence Nicholls, Albert Nicholls and Leonard Kersley, and also charged with causing grievous bodily harm. James Tibbs senior, 44, a scrap metal merchant from Romford, in Essex, was also accused of conspiracy to cause grievous bodily harm, possessing a firearm and ammunition illegally, and conspiring to pervert the course of justice. George Tibbs, 55, was the third member of the Tibbs family to be arrested, but he was only charged with receiving stolen property. Michael Machin, 25, was accused of conspiring with others to cause grievous bodily harm, as was 38-year-old licensee Alexander Cousins, alongside charges of illegal possession of a shotgun. The raids were confined to the London area, where, in the previous few months, there had been a series of bombings and shootings. Witnesses were said to have been terrified and unable to stay in their homes for fear of reprisals should they give evidence against the 12 men. In court, the jury were told how the family of Jimmy Tibbs had imposed a "rule of terror" on a part of East London. Their rule involved three attempted murders, kidnapping and blackmail. The family wove a sickening story of hatred, fear, violence and severe personal injury, claimed prosecuting counsel, Michael Corkery. "The Tibbs family and associates in varying degrees followed a course of conduct designed to impose their rule over parts of the East End of London," he said. The case had come to court after a man named Michael Fawcett tried to break up a fight between Robert Tibbs and another man in a pub in Stepney. Robert Tibbs had produced a knife but, in the struggle, he himself was badly cut on the neck. Tibbs was reported to have shouted at the time: "Some bastard will die for this." Fawcett tried to make peace with the family, but after a meeting with Robert's uncle, George Tibbs, he decided to leave Britain and went to live in Spain. Then, a friend of Fawcett's, Ronald Curtis, was kidnapped. He was picked up outside a pub and pushed into a car after being hit on the head with an iron bar, allegedly by John Tibbs, 24. In the car, professional boxer Jimmy held a knife to the kidnapped man's throat, the point penetrating the skin. Later, when Curtis said Fawcett was in Spain, Tibbs threatened him with a gun.

The first attempted murder was said to involve pub manager Leonard Kersley, who was overheard expressing contempt for the Tibbs family. Tibbs Sr, armed with a chopper, his son John and two other men, Stanley Naylor and Michael Machin, armed with knives, attacked Kersley. He was gashed on the head with the chopper and suffered knife wounds to the body. The court heard that the next attempted murder was of two brothers, Albert and Terence Nicholls, who were attacked after leaving the Rose of Denmark pub in Canning Town. Both were seriously wounded. A witness in the case, which was opened at the Old Bailey in November 1972, was asked in court about his involvement with the Kray twins. Michael Fawcett, 28, claimed he fled to Spain out of fear after a quarrel with the Tibbs family and denied that he had ever worked for the Krays. He did admit to knowing the brothers reasonably well, but he denied trying to collect money from the Tibbs on behalf of the Krays. Having called the Tibbs family "dirty bastards", Leonard Kersley was called to court to testify against them. He told how he had been slashed several times across the face and that he had made his remarks about the family when he had been serving behind the bar at the Black Boy in Stepney. He had been confronted outside his home by John Tibbs and Michael Machin. He had run from his attackers but they easily caught up with him and started slashing at him. Jimmy Tibbs then hit Kersley on the head with the chopper (which was similar to a meat cleaver). James Tibbs Sr had ordered Kersley to make a statement to police to keep his boys out of trouble. By mid-

January 1973, it was all over for the Tibbs family when they were found guilty of the charges brought against them. Their bid to win the territory left behind by the Krays had been smashed. The underworld war in which they had sought to wreak fear and terror proved short-lived when all accused members of the gang were found guilty at the Old Bailey. During the 43-day trial, the jury had heard how the Tibbs gang enforced a rule of terror against its rivals and anyone who offended its members. Its special band of "justice" had meant the use of guns, knives, hatchets, fists and boots. But the war had not all been one way. The vendetta had led to the bombing of Jimmy Tibbs' van – the bomb was linked to the ignition. Six days before this, a bomb had blasted a café and boarding house owned by the Tibbs family. James Tibbs Sr had sought to rule the underworld and had met with some fierce opposition to his plans. However, he was so confident that he openly boasted to the police that he had the power to muzzle any of the witnesses they could bring. The gang members thought they were safe because they believed everyone had a price – either through cash or terror. The press reported that the Tibbs gang made up its own rules in London's tough East End. It did not recognize the law. In members' own violent world, their word was law, and they enforced it ruthlessly.

None of the bombings carried out on the Tibbs gang brought forth information for the police. They were constantly met with a wall of silence, while the Tibbs gang preferred to "take care of their own problems". The Tibbs gang had led a campaign to terrorize parts of the East End and to teach salutary lessons to rivals and all those out of favour. However, the tactics of Wickstead's officers saw Tibbs Sr, his three sons and henchmen sent to prison for a total of 58 years.

Later in January 1973, Scotland Yard's gang-busting squad carried out further raids in a weekend blitz, which saw them seize more than 40 tons of pornographic material with a market value of £400,000. Thirty-eight people, including several women, were detained for questioning. The detectives also seized three printing presses and chained up other printing equipment to stop it from being used. Serious charges were expected to be made against a number of people. Wickstead had turned his attention to pornography distributors because gang warfare had broken out between rival gangs in London's Soho. Feuding began in the early summer of 1972 when two new groups of pornography pedlars started to invade the market controlled by four other gangs. In the weeks leading up to this latest swoop there had been a number of violent clashes and several men had been badly beaten; some had been stabbed. The swoop included finding vast quantities of blue films, obscene books and photographs, and girlie magazines. Fifty premises were raided altogether, while a farmhouse, near Camberley in Surrey, revealed the biggest stash of pornographic material, worth an estimated £250,000.

With the behind-the-scenes involvement of Ronnie and Reggie Kray and other gang leaders, gangs were still big headlines during the 1980s. It wasn't quite the same as the news that had made the press in the 1950s, 1960s and 1970s – there had been shifts – but gang warfare was believed to have been behind a firebomb attack which killed at least seven people in July 1982. The victims were in an illegal gambling den in Gerrard Street, Soho, in the heart of London's Chinatown. There was an explosion in the basement club, then fire swept through the three-storey building above it. Detectives thought that the blast was caused by a petrol bomb thrown in through the door, while members of the Chinese community feared that the attack was the latest in a series of clashes between rival gangs. The gangs involved were reported to be the 14K Triad – the rulers of London's Chinese underworld – and a new gang known as the Singaporeans. One source from the Chinese community said: "We are afraid that there may be more revenge attacks after this." As firemen fought the blaze, a second explosion, probably caused by gas, ripped the building apart. Two policemen were seriously injured and detectives appealed for help from anyone who saw a red Ford Capri with a black vinyl roof driving away just after the firebomb attack.

In 1991 "Mad" Frankie Fraser was back in the press when it was revealed that he had been gunned down outside a nightclub in August. Fraser – described as "hitman for torture boss Charlie Richardson" – was seriously injured in hospital after being shot in the temple and eye. Police feared that the 67-year-old, who, it was reported, used to carry a pair of pliers to deal with the loose-tongued, may have been a victim of gang warfare sweeping South

The fight against gangs and their criminal activities dominated the 20th century. This circa 1905 picture shows a group of Scotland Yard detectives in various disguises before setting out on a special observation mission, which resulted in the important capture of a cunning gang of thieves.

Gang violence in the 21st century is not confined to inter-gang rivalry. In April 2011, paramedics were called to treat a gunshot victim in Clapham, South London, but had to flee when they feared they were the targets of the gangs' shots. By the time it was deemed safe for them to return, the 21-year-old victim had died of his injuries.

Several notorious gang members – such as Frankie Fraser and Paul Ferris – have reinvented themselves and achieved something akin to celebrity status, having written books about their life of crime.

Numerous initiatives have been set up around the country to try to prevent youngsters from getting involved in the downward spiral of gang life. Here, former London Mayor Ken Livingstone visits the Eternal Life Support Centre in Peckham High Street, which runs a programme to encourage at-risk kids to stay away from gang culture and crime.

Thompson Gang Police examine the van in which Patrick Welsh and James Goldie died after being run off the road by Scottish crime boss Arthur Thompson in 1966. The two men were spotted by Thompson shortly after they placed a bomb underneath his car, which killed his mother-in-law, who had been sitting in the passenger seat. He chased the two members of the rival gang and hit their van with his car, causing it to crash into a lamppost, killing them both.

Arthur Thompson – known as the "Godfather" – the notorious Glasgow-born gangster who made his mark on the streets of Scotland in the 1950s, and went on to take charge of organized crime for over 30 years.

Arthur Thompson Senior attends the funeral of his son, who was killed outside the family home, The Ponderosa, on 18th August 1991.

Paul Ferris walks from Glasgow High Court in June 1992, after being found not guilty of the murder of Arthur Thompson Jnr in Scotland's longest murder trial.

Krays The Krays – identical twins Ronnie (left) and Reggie (right) with their older brother Charlie – pictured in 1965. Their gang, the "Firm", was an integral force in 1950s and 1960s London, and was involved in armed robberies, arson, protection rackets, assaults and murders.

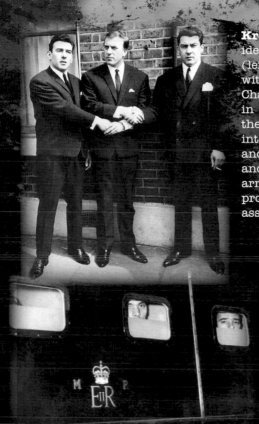

The faces of East End gangland bosses Ronnie and Reggie Kray peer out of a prison van in March 1969 after they had been sentenced to life imprisonment for the murders of George Cornell and Jack "the Hat" McVitie. Brother Charlie received 10 years as an accessory to the murders.

The team who caught the Krays, pictured in March 1969 (from left to right): Detective Daphne Robeson, Detective Carole Liston, Detective Janet Adams, Sergeant A Gallacher, Sergeant A Trevette, Commander John du Rose, Superintendent Leonard Nipper Read, Inspector Frank Cater, Superintendent Henry Mooney and Sergeant Algernon Hemmingway.

Glasgow Frankie Vaughan talks with four Glasgow gang leaders in July 1968; they later pledged to end the gangs' fighting.

Frankie Vaughan visits the Easterhouse Project with local kids in 1977. Concerned by the gang warfare he saw among young people in the late 1960s, Vaughan co-ordinated a successful weapons amnesty and donated the proceeds from his concert at Glasgow Pavilion to help set up the project that still helps young people from Easterhouse today.

Walter Norval, godfather of the Glasgow XYY gang, pictured leaving court with John McDuff and Joseph Polding in 1977.

London In the 1950s, British youth began to forge its own identity through several mediums, one of which was fashion – but being part of a gang could bring more serious issues. This group of Teddy Boys are waiting for their turn in court to face charges of insulting behaviour and carrying offensive weapons.

Jack "Spot" Comer walks down a narrow street in London in August 1955. The gangland leader – who had been a dominant force since the 1930s – found his influence waning by the 1950s and effectively retired. Jack had joined his first gang at the age of seven, when boys from the Jewish side of Myrdle Street fought their Catholic rivals from the other end of the street.

"Mad" Frankie Fraser – along with Bobby Warren – received a seven-year prison sentence for his part in attacking Spot and his then wife, Rita, outside their Paddington home in 1956. Fraser would later become part of the Richardson Gang in the 1960s and would eventually spend 42 years in over 20 different prisons in the UK.

Charlie Richardson led the Richardson Gang with his younger brother Eddie in the 1960s. They had a reputation as two of London's most sadistic gangsters.

Ten-year-old Damilola Taylor was murdered by a gang in 2000, but his memory lives on with a memorial outside the Oliver Goldsmith Primary School and the Damilola Taylor Centre in Peckham, South London.

Billy Hill, king of the Soho underworld, with Albert Dimes, at the funeral of William Blythe in February 1957.

Richard Taylor, father of Damilola, takes centre stage at the *Daily Mirror*'s the People's March "Stop Knives Save Lives" on 20th September 2008 in Hyde Park, London.

Tributes are left at the scene of the murder of 16-year-old Kodjo Yenga, who was fatally stabbed through the heart in Hammersmith Grove, West London, in March 2007.

Authorities have started initiatives to curb the gang culture that is threatening the safety of today's youth. This anonymous former South London gang member was shot in the knee, stabbed seven times and even had his own friend shot in the head during his gang days.

EXECUTIONERS

THE KILLERS

GUILTY: McNee was in gang that gunned down Stirlands

GUILTY: Russell is facing life in jail along with other two thugs

Trio face life over couple's gun deaths

By RODCHAYTOR

A GANG boss and two killers who executed an innocent couple in a revenge attack were last night facing life in jail.

The 39-year-old ringleader – who cannot be named – John Russell and Michael McNee were found guilty of plotting to murder John and Joan Stirland at their seaside hideaway.

They were shot dead just weeks after Joan's son Michael O'Brien, 23, was jailed for murdering a man who was friends with a gang member.

As the trio were led from the dock, it was revealed relatives of the Stirlands are still in fear of their lives despite the convictions.

Joan's daughters, Rosina and Tonette, in their 20s, are being guarded in police safe houses. John's son Lee, 33, and daughter-in-law Adele, 28, are under 24-hour guard.

A family friend said: "Even though three of the gang are now in prison, it isn't over yet. No one is sleeping easy in their beds."

The thugs blasted John, 55, and 51-year-old Joan to death at their home in Trusthorpe, Lincs, where they had fled to escape the gang.

They had snubbed offers of police protection, despite being victims of an earlier gun attack when they lived in Nottingham. Prosecutor

HOME: Where couple died

Tim Spencer told Birmingham crown court the execution was "clinically efficient." He said: "Their vengeance was swift and devastating."

Mr Spencer said Russell, 29, and 29-year-old McNee, both from Nottingham, were either the hitmen or lookouts and got their orders from the gang boss on mobile phones.

The killers struck on August 8, 2004, a few weeks after O'Brien got life for killing Marvyn Bradshaw, 22, outside a Nottingham pub in 2003.

Innocent Marvyn's 19-year-old friend witnessed the murder and, unable to cope, turned to drugs and died of pneumonia a year later.

The gang vowed to avenge both deaths, but could not get to O'Brien in jail. Instead they turned on John and Joan after tracing them to the village where they sought refuge.

A prowler, thought to be Russell, was spotted in the couple's home the night before they were killed. Joan called police next day but by the time officers arrived they were dead.

After the hearing, the couple's family said in a statement: "This was an unnecessary, pointless killing of an innocent, loving couple. It has devastated our lives. We are satisfied with the verdicts but nothing will bring back John and Joan."

Russell, McNee and the gang boss are due to be sentenced today.

Five other men were acquitted of plotting to kill the Stirlands.

r.chaytor@mirror.co.uk

THE VICTIMS

INNOCENT: Joan and John were shot dead

Nottingham John Russell and Michael McNee were found guilty in June 2006 of plotting to murder John and Joan Stirland. The Stirlands had been in hiding but were found executed in a gang-style attack.

Liverpool The grave of murdered youngster Rhys Jones is decked out in Everton colours. The 11-year-old was shot dead crossing the Fir Tree pub car park in Liverpool's Croxteth Park Estate in August 2007.

Police search teams hunt for clues in woodland at the back of the Fir Tree pub, where Rhys Jones was gunned down.

Police seal off an address in Croxteth, Liverpool, where they arrested suspects for the murder of Rhys Jones. Sean Mercer, an 18-year-old member of the Croxteth Crew gang, was convicted and sentenced to life imprisonment, with a recommended minimum term of 22 years.

A sign is nailed to a tree outside Liverpool Crown Court at the start of the second week of the Rhys Jones murder trial.

Dubbed Britain's number one drug dealer, Curtis Warren was facing 14 years in jail in October 2009 for his part in a drugs plot.

The Whitney clan and associates, who were finally brought to justice as their drugs empire was closed down in 2011.

Manchester These stills from CCTV footage provide a real insight into the hatred that exists between rival gangs. Violence flared between Manchester's Gooch Close Gang and Longsight Crew as members were being cared for in different sections of the city's Royal Infirmary in May 2005.

Birmingham This aerial view of the Aston area of Birmingham clearly shows how close the territories of the Burger Bar Boys and the Johnson Crew are. Charlene Ellis, 18, died, and her sister Sophia was wounded, in a hail of automatic gunfire as they stepped out of a party on New Year's Day 2003 for a breath of fresh air. A 17-year-old friend, Letisha Shakespeare, was also killed, and the twins' cousin, Cheryl Shaw, 17, was wounded.

JAILING OF JU-JU MAN
..KING OF THE YARDIES

12 YEARS
Bourne was leader of The Firm

11 YEARS
Leader, 21, was gang member

9 YEARS
Osei-Appiah was also in the mob

12 YEARS
Lambie was feared as a spirit power

'Untouchable' no more

By CHRIS HUGHES

A GANG leader feared as untouchable because he had the voodoo power of "ju ju" was finally locked up yesterday.

Yardie Mr Big Mark Lambie got 12 years for kidnap and torture with three henchmen go to prison with him.

Lambie was No.1 on the wanted list of Scotland Yard's Operation Trident, which targets black-on-black gun crime in London.

The man who at 14 was charged with the Broadwater Farm killing of PC Keith Blakelock may have been behind 14 gangland murders, police think.

Last night Det Insp Peter Lansdown said: "Lambie has been thought to have magical powers.

"There are those that have thought he is a devil, he could not be harmed and he heals up if he is wounded. Some in his community say he has got the 'ju ju' - that his father bought him this supernatural protection.

"Lambie's sentence has destroyed the myth of his invincibility."

He headed the TMD mob - Tottenham Man Dem - which terrorised black communities across the capital.

Fellow crime boss Anthony Bourne, 21, who ran The Firm, also got 12 years at the Old Bailey.

Warren Leader, 21, was given 11 years and Francis Osei-Appiah, also 21, nine years.

Lambie, 31, and Bourne were convicted of kidnap and blackmail offences after an 11-week trial. Bourne was cleared of attempted murder.

Judge Martin Stephens said the four were "violent men who appear

FLAT: Torture 'room'

to consider themselves above the law". The kidnap victims were held in a flat on the same Tottenham estate where PC Blakelock was hacked to death in 1985.

That charge against Lambie was dropped and he got community service for throwing petrol bombs.

Snatched Twaine Morris, 24, and Gregory Smith, 32, were drug dealers with access to cash that their captors wanted, the court was told.

They were tortured with a hammer and electric iron. Boiling water was poured on their genitals.

Morris told the court Lambie was known as the "Obeah-man" - a Jamaican voodoo spirit who walks in darkness.

Police said the pair felt they would die whether they gave evidence or not... "their least chance of dying" was with the support of police. Lambie, of Streatham, South London, who has three children by different women, was once accused over a club shooting.

The victim withdrew his allegation and was charged £10,000 by Lambie for time the gangster spent in jail on remand.

In 1996 Lambie was shot in a gun battle outside a Wembley wine bar but survived.

A year later, would-be assassins sprayed a London restaurant with bullets, leaving one diner paralysed. Lambie was unscathed.

Last night Det Supt Barry Phillips said of its jailing: "This is a tremendous day for the black communities, as will as the police."

c.hughes@mirror.co.uk

Yardies Four Yardies are jailed for their crimes in May 2002. Mark Lambie received 12 years for kidnap and torture, while cohorts Anthony Bourne, Warren Leader and Francis Osei-Appiah were sentenced to between nine and 12 years.

Biker Gangs A policeman stands guard in Cookham, Berkshire, where rival Hell's Angels chapters clashed, resulting in the murder of two men – Colin Hunting and Michael Harrison – in September 1983.

ASSASSINATED

BODY
Dead biker lies on M40, covered by white sheet yesterday

..ON THE M40

Gunman shoots biker in head from passing vehicle

By TRACEY KANDOHLA

A MOTORCYCLIST was shot dead yesterday as he rode his bike along the busy M40 with a group of friends.

The father-clad 51-year-old man was hit in the head by a shot allegedly fired from a vehicle that overtook him.

Witness Paul Roberts told how others drivers screeched to a halt as they spotted the biker lying face-down.

He said: "I was driving to a BMW in the fast lane. The car ahead veered into my lane. I had to brake. A man in a car in the middle lane pulled out and overtook me and I glanced over and there was a biker lying face-down on the floor.

Hell's Angel Gerry Tobin was shot dead by a rival gang member as he rode his bike along the M40 after a rock festival in August 2007.

Authorities were concerned in January 2013 that rival biker gangs would bring their turf wars to the United Kingdom.

BIKER GANGS BRING WAR TO BRITAIN

Cops fear clashes as crews roll into Europe

By JOHN ROBINSON

THE FIGHT RIDERS

London in the early 1990s. His nephew, David Brindle, 23, had been shot dead two weeks previously in The Bell pub in Walworth (at the heart of Fraser's old patch). In gang-member style, Fraser kept quiet about the attack and Scotland Yard said: "He doesn't want to know us." The gangster – once one of the UK's most feared men – was hit as he left the Turnmills Club in Clerkenwell Road, London, with his fiancée Marilyn Wisbey, daughter of Great Train robber Tommy Wisbey. The underworld was bracing itself for a revenge attack and one source stated: "No one can believe The Old Man has been shot. Someone will pay for this." The attack came five years after Fraser was released from prison after serving 20 years for his part in the Richardson gang torture trial.

In 2004, a 24-year-old accountant was shot by a gang bullet in the chest, but survived when it ricocheted off the underwire in her bra. Helen Kelly collapsed to the ground and thought she was dying, but the bullet had been deflected by the underwire through her breast and out of her body. The stray shot had hit Helen as rival gangs fought a gun battle in a central London street. In October 2005, 28-year-old Linton Ambursley, from Lewisham, southeast London, was jailed for 12 years at the Old Bailey after admitting wounding with intent over the attack. Tyrone Headley, also 28, of New Cross, was jailed for two years for assisting an offender. Helen was shot in November 2004 just after moving to the capital from her native Tyneside. She had unknowingly been caught in a fight between the Ghetto Boys from Peckham and a rival crew from Bermondsey as they clashed outside the Urban

Music Awards at the Barbican Centre. "There was a lot of blood on my stomach," said Helen, who relived the event for the court case, "but, I didn't know where it was coming from." The young woman spent three days in hospital and took three weeks off work to recover. She was extremely lucky to be alive.

Two years later, two brothers were named for the first time in the shocking murder of a child. The victim was 10-year-old Damilola Taylor, who was murdered by a gang, the Young Peckham Boys, in 2000. Damilola had been seen on CCTV skipping along as he left a library in Peckham, just minutes before his death. Four youths were accused of murder after stabbing the schoolboy in the leg with a broken bottle. Damilola was left to bleed to death on a stairwell in Peckham. The two brothers, Danny and Ricky Preddie, were to stand trial accused of manslaughter. They had been cleared of murder and causing grievous bodily harm with intent to rob in a trial that ended in April 2006, but they had previously been granted anonymity because Danny Preddie was only 17 at the time of the trial. At the first trial in 2002, the key prosecution witness was discredited, so a fresh investigation was launched by Scotland Yard and the brothers charged after new forensic evidence was uncovered. Damilola's blood was found on the sweatshirt and trainers of the two brothers and they were accused of stabbing the 10-year-old to death. Jurors were told in June 2006 that new evidence provided a "compelling" case against the Preddie brothers and showed they killed Damilola with a broken bottle. Prosecutor Victor Temple, QC, said: "The evidence points with certainty to their criminal involvement." The clues were missed by forensic experts during the original police probe. The brothers, who were 12 and 13 at the time of the attack, denied manslaughter. A witness – who had to fight off the sexual advances of a juror in the case, who was then discharged – told the re-formed jury that he had talked with Ricky Preddie at a children's home after the 10-year-old was stabbed. He asked Preddie if he had juked (stabbed) the boy and the alleged reply came: "Yeah man, I did it." In August 2006 a girl indecently assaulted by Damilola's killers spoke of how Danny and Ricky Preddie thought they were "untouchable". The girl, who was 12 years old at the time of the sex attack, was pinned to the ground by the brothers, who ripped off her clothes. She said: "They ran around calling themselves The Untouchables because they committed so many crimes and got away with it." The girl, who wasn't named for legal reasons, was one of many victims of the Preddies' gang, the Young Peckham Boys. Others included boys beaten with baseball bats and train commuters robbed at knifepoint. The girl and her friend were ambushed in a park in 1999, a year before the murder. The gang started to touch the girls and they began screaming. "They dragged us to the floor and grabbed hold of me and took my clothes off. I was screaming but they didn't care," said the girl. The assault by the Preddies and three other boys – who were later cleared of killing Damilola during the first trial in 2002 – ended only when the mum of one of the girls found them. She called the police, but was warned off by the gang. The girl's home was firebombed, and a gang went round and started shouting, terrifying the family inside. There were threatening phone calls and the gang also broke into the girl's house and wrecked it. The second girl was so traumatized that she fled to Ireland. The Preddies and their accomplices were charged with indecent assault and sent to the Crown Court. However, the judge ruled that they should have been sent to a youth court and halted the case, fearing a jury trial would breach their human rights. This was another time when the brothers got away with their crimes. They remained free to terrorize the North Peckham Estate and this ultimately led to the death of Damilola Taylor. In June 2000, Danny Preddie was convicted of hitting a 13-year-old boy with a baseball bat after demanding money. In 1999, Ricky was given a 12-month supervision order for carrying a bladed article. The brothers were initially eliminated from the Damilola inquiry, but by the time Danny was rearrested he had committed 24 crimes, including burglary and robbing commuters at knifepoint. The Preddies and the four other boys, who could not be named in 2006, formed the core of the gang, demanding cash, trainers and mobile phones from teenagers. The brothers were compared by a police chief to "organized criminals". Rod Jarman said: "This group of young people understands how the systems work and are extremely effective at undermining the investigation of crime, undermining witnesses and victims." Anyone who stood up to the gang got a "juking" – a stab to the thigh with a knife or broken glass. Tragically for Damilola, the gang believed that the injury would not kill.

Damilola's brave parents, Richard and Gloria Taylor, spoke of their relief in 2006, when their son's killers were brought to justice. They said that no trial could bring back their son but they also said: "We pray that his gentle soul can rest in peace." It had been a hugely difficult six years for Damilola's family, but it was finally brought to an end in a small way when Danny and Ricky Preddie were found guilty of manslaughter. The gangster brothers – as the press described them – had a string of convictions. In stark contrast to the quiet dignity shown in court by the Taylors, Ricky Preddie ranted from the dock as he learned his fate at the Old Bailey. He yelled hysterically: "You must be crazy! Guilty? I'm innocent. F***ing stitch up! You f***ing police, you're gonna pay. You f***ing c***s!" As his brother Danny tried to calm him, he broke down in tears. Ricky was dragged, still screaming, to the cells by 10 guards. Danny remained, looking dazed and in shock. The brothers were remanded in custody for reports before sentencing, but they could expect to be jailed for life, or so people believed. Gloria and Richard Taylor impressed all they met following their son's tragic death with their dignity and fortitude. In a poignant legacy to his young son's death, Mr Taylor released a letter asking youngsters to make a written pledge not to carry knives. The letter said: "Together we can turn the tide on weapon-assisted crime." Damilola Taylor bled to death from a severed artery when he was stabbed with the bottle. At the time, Danny was meant to be under 24-hour curfew at a children's home, while Ricky was also being monitored by the probation service. It is believed that Danny slipped out of his hostel through a window and used the timekeeping log as an alibi.

It took the jury six hours and 20 minutes to find the Preddie brothers guilty. However, the brothers got just eight years each for stabbing a child to death. For the Taylors it was just another in a long catalogue of failures and a huge disappointment. Would these short sentences deter other youngsters committing gang-related crimes? Doubtful. The gang members showed no remorse for their victim. The length of their sentences just seemed to reinforce what they possibly believed all along: they hadn't really done anything wrong.

In 2007, the grieving mum of a lad of 16 murdered by schoolchildren sobbed as she asked: "Why did they kill my precious boy?" Ladjua Yenga's son, Kodjo, was stabbed to death by a 10-strong mob in school uniform, urged on by girls screaming: "Kill him. Kill him!" It was feared that the gentle, churchgoing student fell victim to the vicious Murder Dem Pussies gang, which, in March 2007, sent a taunting rap to the mobile phones of Kodjo's friends. The lyrics ran: "You'll never catch us, we're MDP. MDP you faces gets mashed. Mess with us and you face gets slashed. Don't test us or your body gets slinged [stabbed] with." Two boys of 14 and 16 were held by police on 16th March; the police also continued to quiz seven other boys, four of whom were 13, two 15 and one 21. Ladjua, who had moved to the UK from the Conga for a better life for her son, wept at her home in

Ladbroke Grove, West London, and said: "Kodjo was a beautiful boy, very polite and loving. I loved him so much." Kodjo had been an ambitious student who studied hard and wanted to make something of his life. He had wanted to be a success working in television and design. Meanwhile, Kodjo's friends were convinced that the MDP gang, which had 100 members at the time, was behind the killing. One girl, simply named as Kirsty (too afraid to give her full name to the papers), said: "They want to fight and kill you." She went on to say that if youngsters didn't want to fight gang members, they were called "a pussy". The gang was known to terrorize the area and threaten to kill, if members were even looked at in the "wrong" way. Most members of the gang were known to own Staffordshire bull terriers. Kodjo was walking his own bull terrier when he was attacked. One theory was that the gang wanted to steal his dog. His friends gathered at a makeshift memorial near the murder scene, where they stood in silence as they listened to the MDP's rap on a mobile phone. Kodjo, known to friends as Kizzle, was stabbed in the heart in Hammersmith Grove after being beaten with poles. His 15-year-old girlfriend, Cookie, who clasped him as he lay dying, said: "He's in my heart for life ... I have to be strong as that's what he'd want." Kodjo was the fourth London teenager to be murdered in six weeks. He was in the band Ride for Life, which sings anti-knife lyrics. In a tribute on the band's website, the band said: "Kizzle will be missed by his family, friends and Cookie ... One day we will reunite. Kizzle rest in peace." The teenager was studying for four

AS-levels at St Charles Catholic Sixth Form College in Ladbroke Grove. Police said of the murder: "This was a meaningless and despicable crime. The boy's family is absolutely devastated."

The scene was a far cry from that of the professionals sitting at the wooden tables outside Chez Kristof, shielding their eyes from the spring sunshine as they sipped skinny cappuccinos just a street away. Here, young mums strolled out of million-pound houses pushing Mamas & Papas pushchairs past rows of BMWs and Golf convertibles. A young woman in a pink pashmina and oversized sunglasses walked her pet spaniel down Hammersmith Grove chatting loudly into her mobile about plans for a dinner party. At the corner of Richford Street, however, on 17th March 2007, the scene of teenage mourners and an ever-growing carpet of flowers tells a different story. Less than 24 hours earlier, 16-year-old Kodjo Yenga lay on this spot bleeding to death. The boy's school friends had been arriving all day. Some to lay flowers, others just to stand and look in silence. Kate Jackson, writing in the *Mirror*, described how "the eerie calm was in stark contrast to the previous evening when Kodjo's teenage attackers chased him down the street yelling threats before he was stabbed. Kodjo wasn't in a gang – he belonged to a non-violent band." Melvyn Davis, director of the Male Development Service, which runs programmes for disaffected young people, said: "Why are our young people so violent, why are they joining gangs and what can be done to change the situation?" He believed that much of their behaviour was symptomatic of their environment, as well as a failure of adults to both listen and protect them. "We have to wake up to the need to address the insurgency that is happening not in Iraq, but within our neighbourhoods," he stated. One local 16-year-old girl said that gang warfare was rife in the area. She cited that there were around 60 or 70 members of the MDP, who, it was claimed, had earned "respect" because of the actions they carried out, including robberies. Most of the MDP were aged around 13 to 15, but there was also an older set belonging to the gang who were aged between 21 and 31 and who had all reportedly been in prison. The gang's "big" thing was breeding dogs, although members were very cruel to the animals. They then sold the dogs to buy drugs or guns. One young girl said that the motive for the attack on Kodjo was possibly revenge. He had been seen dancing at a rave called Sexy Love with a girl from a rival gang known as the RBS. The MDP were also reported not to like the Ride for Life (RFL) crew because they were "too nice". Ladbroke Grove was thought to have around 200 gang members in the locality in 2007. The MDP were the biggest, followed by the Black Stars, GBH, Y2K and RBS, spanning the Fulham, Acton and Hammersmith areas of West London.

At this point in time, becoming a gang member often involved an initiation test, such as mugging a person on the street or carrying out a robbery. A 16-year-old friend of Kodjo's said that many people joined gangs because they liked the status and others joined because it ensured their safety. The girl believed that many of those involved didn't have fathers, or didn't receive a great deal of love at home. "They get into a gang and they feel part of something," she said. Another witness revealed that the Ride for Life crew had come under a number of attacks. One boy was bricked and another had boiling water thrown in his face. Melvyn Davis added: "The journey from nursery school to being a knife-wielding, gun-toting hoodie on the street corner is all too common. Although laws have been tightened around domestic violence the provision for children who are also victims is non-existent. Many young boys and girls are living in families where their basic needs have not been met. Young people see themselves as soldiers fighting against society and each other. How bad does it need to get before we regard it as a civil war?" However, some people were trying to make a difference.

In April 2007, it was reported that reformed criminal Junior Smart, 31, had saved more than £3 million by persuading some of Britain's worst teenage gangsters to give up their life of crime. He had already helped 16 young offenders to change their lives with his groundbreaking mentoring work when reporters caught up with him. He visited gangsters in prison to persuade them to give up their life of crime and he acted as a mentor when they were released. Youth worker Junior had been at the helm of the Southwark Offenders Support Project, run by charity St Giles Trust, since it was set up towards the end of 2006. Based in South London, the charity was right at the heart of the community most affected by gang warfare and murder at the time. Junior knew what it was like to be a prisoner. He had been sentenced to 12 years for a drug-related offence and towards the end of his sentence (reduced to 10 years) he started doing community work. One of the young offenders that Junior helped, and who turned his life around, was a former member of the East Dulwich Soldiers and the Young Peckham Boys. The 20-year-old – who wasn't named – had already been jailed five times for violent offences. He was hopeful in 2007 that Junior's influence would help him reform for the long-term future. But even in 2007 this young man was shocked by the gun crime that was beginning to infiltrate London's streets. He said: "Kids on the estates don't think they're going to live until they're 18. There's no hope, so no one has any great plans for the future." Meanwhile, later that same year, Damilola's killers failed in their appeal to have their sentences cut. And, in April 2008, Richard Taylor lost his wife Gloria to a heart attack. It was a tragic end to a family that had fought so valiantly, yet with dignity, to bring their son's killers to justice. They had remained strong and found great love and strength in each other. The couple had also set up the Damilola Taylor Trust.

Ricky Preddie was eventually sent back to jail, after his release in 2010, for breaching the terms of his curfew and licence conditions, which included not returning to Peckham in South London. In 2011, the former gang leader was spotted in the area and police feared that he was trying to make contact with his old gang members.

An article in March 2012, some five years after the death of

Kodjo, summed up the extent of the damage carried out by 62 of the worst London gangs. According to reports, these 62 profiled gangs were responsible for 22 per cent of serious violence, 17 per cent of all robberies, 50 per cent of shootings and 14 per cent of rapes in the capital. Tom Parry, writing in the *Mirror*, said: "Staring me squarely in the eye, Ali casually brushes off his chances of being shot dead as an occupational hazard." A street gang member at the age of 14, Ali exposed the true scale of Britain's gang crisis to the journalist when he said: "To be honest, you're going to die one day; it's just one of them, isn't it?" Ali, who still lived with his parents in Nottingham at the time, had decided that being a drug-dealing foot soldier for a local criminal network was his career choice. The gang came first. He added: "My mum has been crying on my shoulder telling me I'm taking too many risks. She tells me I could get shot any time." Ali is part of a severe epidemic in Britain's inner cities in which boys as young as eight are being coerced to join older street thugs. A 10.6 per cent increase in serious youth violence in the six months to October 2011 had been linked to gangs. Sitting opposite the journalist, with his hood up to disguise his identity, Ali told Tom Parry about his day-to-day life. "My mate has already been shot four times," he said. It turned out the mate in question was only just walking again after the fourth shooting. "That's just the life we know. Last week, even his little brother got shot at," he stated calmly. "I only carry a knife if there's a real threat. I hide it in my belt," he continued. Another threat is kidnapping.

Many gang members are routinely kidnapped over money or for selling drugs in the wrong location. Schoolboys like Ali are drawn in by older gang leaders with diamonds in their teeth, according to Parry. "When I meet Ali, he unfurls a wad of £10 notes tucked inside his jacket. He has come into the city to get his 'grillz', gold caps fitted over four of his front teeth," Parry wrote. The bill is more than £1,000. The bling will win Ali respect, so the cost is well worth it, according to the gang member. Despite the fact that Ali is just 5ft 6in tall, there is an air of menace about him, according to Parry, and a single-mindedness about his "work". Parry found it difficult to believe that the boy in front of him, whose face was just beginning to sprout stubble, was so casual about violence. "I was very young when I first got involved," Ali said. "I had only just started secondary school." He continued: "It all starts with where you grow up and looking to your elders and thinking, 'I want that lifestyle. I want that big gold chain that they got. I want that flashy car; I want them flashy clothes they got.' It will start from street robberies to house robberies to drugs. Some of the elders would just say: 'Don't you want to jump on this? There's more money in this than there is in that.' I've sold coke, E and heroin. Weed (cannabis) is really minor. If you're doing it from scratch you're only making a couple of hundred quid a day, but you can make a grand a day shotting food (selling hard drugs)." Parry wrote that, in an unguarded moment, Ali showed a paranoid mind. Asked if he has a girlfriend, he replied: "Me, I don't trust no female. I keep myself to myself. They could set you up." More than 150 miles away, in East London, the story of former child gangster, Taylor, is similar.

Now 15 years old, he started hanging around with a gang on a notorious estate in Leyton when he was just eight. In 2012, he had to leave his family and flee the area to avoid retribution. Taylor said: "I started out holding on to drugs and knives for the older gang members when they were getting chased." He continued: "They knew the police wouldn't search someone so young." As a thank you for his efforts, Taylor would be paid a few pounds. It was the start of a slippery slope and, from a few pounds for keeping gang members' items safe, he was sucked into gang culture. He would go around his local neighbourhood on his bike carrying a lot of drugs and cash. Most nights he was out until midnight. It didn't matter that it was a school night, or that he had to be up in the morning. On the day that Parry met Taylor, he visited the boy's old turf, where the journalist found about 20 youths in hoodies gathered on a street corner, under a railway bridge. Suddenly, a people carrier arrived, a hand emerged from the vehicle, something was handed over and then the car drove away. In 2012, the Met's new anti-gang squad arrested 315 suspected gang members. According to Scotland Yard, at this time there were 250 gangs in the capital, each with several hundred members. Of them, 62 were considered dangerous. Many of the rape victims in the capital were teenage girls "used and abused within gangs". Detective Allan Davis, speaking in 2012, said: "Gang warfare spills on to the streets sporadically, as when Seydou Diarrassouba, 18, was stabbed to death in front of horrified Oxford Street shoppers on Boxing Day."

It was thought that Seydou was a member of the ABM (All 'Bout Money or All 'Bout Murder) gang based in Stockwell, and had been spotted by enemies in the O-Tray One, or 031 Bloods, gang. Taylor then explained: "All the different circles in different estates would be part of the same postcode gang. Rivalry starts over petty situations and jealousy. Leyton might have had a bit of drama with another area over clothes or money and this could easily escalate into stabbings." In Croydon, Surrey (now Greater London), one of the flashpoints of the riots in the summer of 2011, Parry met 13-year-old James. Small with blond hair and impish features, he was described as an ideal recruit because police would never target him. "Three older boys said I should join their gang," he stated. "They wanted me to look after things for them so they wouldn't get caught. I was really afraid. I didn't think I would get away. I was surrounded, and I was followed a few times after that." He was lucky. David Mitchell, who runs the Gang Avoidance Project in Nottingham, says that many school-age gang recruits are made to look after drugs and weapons with no firm promise of being accepted. However, once they are involved, the financial rewards can be huge. "They believe there is nothing else out there," said Mitchell. "Some can easily make £4,000 a week." Also in 2012, a US-style initiative in London was launched to dissuade schoolchildren from joining gangs. It offered them a way out – or immediate police action. Waltham

Forest Council leader, Chris Robbins, said that the £3.5 million Enough is Enough Project was getting results. Waltham Forest had its fair share of youngsters involved in criminal activities from a young age and the council is often approached by mothers of those youngsters in trouble. The Prince's Trust Team Programme is also helping to tackle Britain's gang problems. It has helped the likes of Arfan Naseer turn their back on gang life and become an example to other youths. Arfan joined a gang in his hometown of Bradford when he was 15 and became a street drug dealer. Six years later, he was jailed for nine years for Class A drugs offences and gang affiliation. While in prison, he took part in the programme and his commitment impressed his tutors. On release, "Naz", as Arfan is also known, was offered the chance to work for Prince Charles' youth charity. He was the first ex-prisoner to do so. While Arfan had been involved in drug dealing, many of his mates had become involved in armed robberies. However, Arfan's prison sentence made a number of his peers think about what it was they were actually doing.

Today, in London, further initiatives in helping dissuade youngsters from joining gangs include a faith-based charity, XLP. Founded by Patrick Regan in 1996, in Peckham, South London, in response to a stabbing in a local school, the eXceL Project (XLP) is at the cutting edge of urban youth work. The charity works with young people from all areas (and they do not have to have any faith or beliefs) to meet social, educational and behavioural needs. XLP believes in empowering these young individuals in order to help them make wise lifestyle choices and realize their potential. In January 2013, XLP held a sell-out one-day conference entitled Tackling Britain's Gang Culture, aimed at understanding the tragic teenage deaths and gang violence that dominate the media. The conference, involving young people, parents, police, former gang members and policymakers, was designed to discuss issues that concern gang culture while asking that all-important question: "How do we bring about change?"

Nottingham

Twenty-seven Teddy Boys "went berserk in a peaceful, sleepy village on a carnival night and terrorized the inhabitants for nearly three hours", a court was told on 12th September 1957. The boys marched through the village "like thugs", claimed a newspaper report, swinging heavily studded belts and chains above their heads. All 27 were charged with threatening behaviour and 12 were also charged with carrying offensive weapons. One was alleged to be the gang leader and was additionally charged with stealing a hat.

Mr H Brewer, prosecuting, said that as soon as the boys were seen in the village, a carnival dance was cancelled. He added that the boys took complete control of a traffic island in the centre of the village, Sandiacre in Derbyshire. A crowd of more than 2,000 people, in the village for the carnival, began to get hostile as the boys challenged police to fight them or arrest them. At about 10pm the Teddy Boys scrambled on a bus for Nottingham, after pushing aside a queue of people. When a police sergeant arrived at the bus stop, one of the men stood at the top of the bus stairs kicking out as the sergeant tried to persuade him to leave the bus. The man in question was Charles O'Leary, 19, of Waterloo Road, Hyson Green, Nottingham, who "appeared" to be the gang leader. The police ordered the bus to be driven to a police station. There, O'Leary was removed from the bus and the rest of the gang "gave up". The bus was then searched and three knuckledusters, one broken bottle and one bottle on a string were found, along with one Commando-type knife and a spiked bottle opener. O'Leary told the court: "Some of the local Teddy Boys had done something to some of my mates the previous Saturday, and we came to get our own back." The 27 men were fined a total of £635 and ordered to pay £21 10s 9d in costs.

While Nottingham has been the scene of much violent crime over the decades, a shocking story was revealed in August 2004. The mother of killer Michael O'Brien shopped her son to police before she and her husband were gunned down themselves the following year. While her son was on the run from police, Joan Stirland told officers where they could find him after he shot innocent Marvyn Bradshaw in 2003. Joan, 53, and her husband John, 55, were murdered at their seaside bungalow in early August 2004, just minutes after calling the police about a prowler. It was believed that the couple were killed in a revenge attack for Mrs Stirland's son's crime.

Joan Stirland had been afraid of her own son. He had routinely beaten her up and she was frightened of him. While O'Brien was hiding out at a mate's flat following the murder he committed, he had spoken to his mother on the phone. At the subsequent trial, a source close to O'Brien did not believe that anyone would have known that Joan Stirland had shopped her own son to police. There were times that Joan Stirland was so frightened of her son that she had to call the police to protect her. O'Brien was jailed for life in July 2004 for the murder of Marvyn Bradshaw.

Mr and Mrs Stirland were so concerned about the life Michael O'Brien was mixed up in that they fled their Nottingham home early in 2004. They had received a number of death threats and decided to move to Trusthorpe, Lincolnshire, where they lived under false names. The police believed that the couple were spotted on a trip to Skegness. They were then traced by the gang, and killed by two men wearing boiler suits and baseball hats. Joan had called Nottingham police at 2pm on the day she was murdered to report a prowler – seen by a neighbour the previous evening. She told police that she had not reported the prowler to Lincolnshire police as she did not want to raise suspicion about who she was. Mrs Stirland asked the police to treat the matter as routine as she did not want the backgrounds of her and her husband revealed locally. The killers, however, must have already been on the scene as, at 2.30pm, their blazing car was found two miles away from the Stirlands' hideaway home. Both Mr and Mrs Stirland were found executed in a gang-style attack.

Three weeks later, a youth aged 19 was questioned by police investigating the suspected revenge murder of the couple. Michael O'Brien had murdered Marvyn Bradshaw, 22, in a case of mistaken identity. It was after this that O'Brien's parents had fled their home in Nottingham. Marvyn Bradshaw's best friend, Jamie Gunn, 19, also died around this time from health-related issues; it was said that he had lost the will to live following the death of his close friend. Police believed that the Stirlands may have been killed as an act of vengeance for the two men's deaths. Although the 19-year-old was in custody in Nottingham, he was due to be questioned in Lincolnshire.

In March 2006 the couple were gunned down in a gangland execution in revenge for a murder their son committed, the court was told. Joan Stirland and her husband John had fled their home after an earlier attempt to kill them. But the gang traced them to the former holiday camp chalet where they hid out, and murdered them in "a calculated, ruthless and merciless execution", the prosecution claimed. The feud began when Michael O'Brien shot Marvyn Bradshaw dead outside a pub in Nottingham. Two weeks later the couple's home in the city was attacked by two helmeted motorcyclists, who blasted the windows late at night with a shotgun and a handgun. The couple fled the following day, changing their address twice before settling in Trusthorpe, Lincs. But the gang became even more determined when Jamie Gunn died of pneumonia. He had been "broken" by witnessing the death of his friend, and died a year later. Prosecutor Tim Spencer, QC, told Birmingham Crown Court they could not easily get at O'Brien, by then jailed for life, but he added: "They could and did easily get at Michael O'Brien's mother and her husband. Their vengeance was swift and devastating." On 8th August 2004 – five days after Jamie Gunn's death – two men with .38 Beretta handguns burst into the couple's bungalow and opened fire. The jury saw police video of the scene taken the next morning. John Stirland, wearing only grey shorts, was slumped over a settee in the living room. He had been shot six times in the back. A TV in the room was still on. Joan, wearing a white top and brown shorts, was lying on her side between the bed and the wall in a bedroom, shot four times. There were blood smears and bullet holes in the wall. Mr Spencer said they had been killed in a "clinical and efficient" manner. He added: "The targets were located quickly and shot just as quickly – an indication of a well-organized, well-planned gang operation.

"The gunmen were seen entering and seen leaving. They entered swiftly and left swiftly. They parked their getaway car close by." The gunmen sped from the scene in a black VW Passat, stolen a week earlier from Nottingham. At an isolated spot four miles away, they set the car ablaze to destroy forensic evidence and were driven away by accomplices. Eight men from Nottingham were accused of conspiring to murder the couple. Mr Spencer claimed: "These defendants are not the whole gang, but a great part of the gang which planned, organized and carried out these shootings.

"It was revenge because of Bradshaw's shooting. It was revenge because of Michael O'Brien's defiance and lack of respect for them. But principally, it was revenge because Bradshaw's friend had died." John Russell, 29, Michael McNee, 20, Shane Bird, 38, Kevin Holm, 38, Andrew McKinnon, 21, Lanelle Douglas, 20, and a 38-year-old man and a 40-year-old man who could not be named for legal reasons, all denied the charge.

By June 2006, the gang boss and two killers who executed the couple were facing life in jail. The 39-year-old gang leader

– who could not be named – John Russell and Michael McNee were found guilty of plotting to murder John and Joan Stirland at their hideaway. It transpired that Bradshaw had been friends with a gang member. As the trio were led from the dock it was revealed that relatives of the murdered couple were still in fear of their lives, despite the conviction. Joan's daughters, Rosina and Tonette, both in their 20s, were being guarded in police safe houses. John's son Lee, 33, and daughter-in-law, Adele, 28, were under 24-hour guard. A family friend said: "Even though three of the gang are now in prison, it isn't over yet. No one is sleeping easy in their beds." The gang had caught up with the couple after Joan and John had refused police protection, despite the earlier gun attack on their home in Nottingham. Russell and McNee were cited as either the hitmen or the lookouts, and got their orders from the gang boss on mobile phones. The gang had openly vowed to avenge the deaths of Bradshaw and Gunn. The prowler spotted by a neighbour of the Stirlands the night before they were executed was said to be Russell. He was actually inside the couple's home when he was spotted. But police were not called until the following afternoon. Five other men were acquitted of plotting to kill Joan and John Stirland.

The gang boss, drug baron Colin Gunn, was jailed for 35 years on 30th June 2006. He was described by Justice Colman Treacy as "ruthless, remorseless and utterly evil". Gangsters Russell and McNee, who helped the crime boss plot the shootings, were locked up for 30 years and 25 years. The judge said: "These were shocking murders by any standards. They were nothing less than the execution of two innocent people. The Stirlands were killed in their own home for no reason other than that one of the victims was the mother of a man you wanted revenge on.

"You could not get to that person directly, so you carefully planned these murders to get to him by proxy." The gang boss was hauled out of the dock at Birmingham Crown Court before sentencing and led to the cells after he hurled abuse at the judge.

In a previous incident, ruthless gangster, Colin Gunn, with a sinister grin on his face, began toying with his cigarette lighter – ignoring his terrified victim's pleas for mercy. The man – a suspected police "grass" – had been doused in petrol by one of Gunn's gang members and feared an agonizing death from first-degree burns. Escape was not an option. His left hand had been nailed to a table. This is a true story. Not disputed by the police. Nor did they dispute similar tales of others who offended Gunn. Many of these victims were taken to the same remote location, had their hands spread out on a table and their knuckles shattered with a hammer. If they struggled, their other hand was smashed too. Certainly it was in 40-year-old Gunn's interests that such stories were spread around the Bestwood Estate in north Nottingham. It was from here he ran his drugs ring – and the estate was held in a grip of fear for two decades. Apart from six murders and at least one unsolved "disappearance", police believe at least 54 non-fatal shootings up to 2005 could be linked to Gunn's gang. But now the underworld boss'

Kray-like reign of terror, which encompassed murder, shootings and punishment beatings, was over.

Gunn is currently in Belmarsh Prison for masterminding the murders of Joan and John Stirland. He was sentenced to nine years for corrupting two police officers. His 42-year-old brother, David, with whom he ran his empire of evil, is in prison for running amphetamines. And up to a dozen gang members were also behind bars in 2007. Free of their influence, life began to return to normal on Bestwood, although drugs-inspired petty pilfering – once strictly controlled by the gang – did return. It was well known that in the early days of Colin Gunn's criminal existence, if someone had their DVD player nicked they could go to him and he would sort it. The culprit would be swiftly identified and the property returned. "Appropriate for Nottingham, they saw themselves [the Gunns] as latter-day Robin Hoods, outlaws administering their own form of justice. There are a few who mourn their passing, but most people are relieved. They were evil, cruel and vicious men," says one local care worker. Born and raised on Bestwood Estate, Gunn was in trouble with the law by the time he was 14, and in youth custody five years later for crimes including violence, burglary, theft, criminal damage and driving offences. A police source said: "He had a typical criminal background. Broken home, allowed to run wild, bunking off school, minor crime, making contacts at the Young Offenders Institution, body-building inside, release, steroids, more weights, more serious criminal activity, back inside, more contacts. A criminal career is born."

A muscular 6ft 4ins, and with the backing of his equally vicious older brother, David, Gunn got out of prison and began to take over Bestwood in the early 1990s. Starting with protection and extortion, he soon turned to drug peddling. By the late Nineties, he began to use guns and extreme violence to wrest control of the heroin trade in north Nottingham. Apart from drugs contacts his influence did not extend beyond the city. But his gang's efforts blighted Nottingham's economy and caused a drop in applications to its university as worried parents advised their children to steer clear of "Shottingham". The county's police were too slow to wake up to the fact that he was out of control. Privately, they did admit that they were possibly preoccupied with other unrelated shootings and they took their eye off the ball as Colin Gunn came to power. Soon the brothers had built up a network of around 30 people who would do their bidding, controlling everything that moved in Bestwood. When a *Mirror* reporter went to knock on doors there in August 2004, there was no reply, but eyes were watching. Within moments of arriving, the journalist and photographer were surrounded by gang members sporting tattoos. The pair managed to retreat to the safety of the photographer's car, but, as they drove away, the door panels were kicked. Around the same time, an all-female TV crew found themselves surrounded by menacing gang members, who poured from the back of a white van brandishing baseball bats, after they ventured into Bestwood. Although Gunn operated from a modest bungalow in the area, he and his brother owned Porsche 4x4s and other flashy vehicles. Gunn's personalized number plate was POWER.

For a time, it seemed his gang was beyond the law. Bent police – one believed to have been deliberately inserted into the Nottinghamshire Force – kept him advised of police movements against him. And potential witnesses and informers were terrified of coming forward, believing he would identify them through his inside men. Acting on information from corrupt police, Gunn once beat up his girlfriend, Vicky Garfoot – the mother of one of his three children – believing she had a conviction for prostitution. In fact, due to a misspelling on the police national computer, Garfoot had someone else's crime registered against her name. Not even the police were safe. At the height of their power, the Gunns let it be known they had taken out a contract on the force's then crime chief, Det Chief Supt Phil Davies. A top detective told a reporter: "One thing is certain, you didn't disrespect Colin Gunn. I wouldn't."

One person who did "diss" Gunn was killer Michael O'Brien – with appalling consequences. O'Brien had murdered Bradshaw, an acolyte of Gunn's, following a drugs turf row. The intended victim had been Jamie Gunn, nephew of Colin and David, who was in the front passenger seat of the vehicle sat outside The Sporting Chance pub in Bulwell. Jamie Gunn not only witnessed the shooting, but ended up with fragments of Bradshaw's brain all over him. He was traumatized and went into a decline, fuelled by the drugs from which his uncles were building a multi-million-pound fortune. During his trial, O'Brien had shouted from the dock to Colin Gunn, who was eyeballing him, that there was "one coming for you" – meaning a bullet. When Jamie Gunn died just days after O'Brien was jailed, Colin Gunn called a "meeting". Several attempts to get at O'Brien behind bars failed, but the main business of the meeting – how to take revenge on the jailed man – continued. Bent BT engineers who were on the payroll traced Joan and John Stirland to Lincolnshire. Gunn's finger wasn't on the trigger, but mobile phone evidence placed him in Trusthorpe the previous evening on a recce mission. Now locked up until his mid-70s, Gunn, according to reports, has not changed. At Christmas 2006, he pulped a fellow inmate, a terror suspect, just for sport. In the end, it took a superhuman effort by police, including 81 separate operations, to bring down his empire. Operation Utah targeted Gunn while Operation Salt went after the bent police. The police on the right side of the law proved that the Gunn gang was not untouchable.

A report after Gunn was sent to jail outlined the fact that the protection given to Joan and John Stirland had been inadequate. It had been suggested previously that the couple had shunned police protection; however, it emerged much later that the couple had never really had the situation explained to them. The report concluded that Mr and Mrs Stirland had been badly let down by the police. Meanwhile, Colin Gunn found Facebook a convenient way to threaten his enemies from the top security prison where he is being held. Because of this, his social networking site was shut down in February 2010. He said in one post: "I will be home one day and I can't wait to look into certain people's eyes and see the fear." Prisoners are banned from using social networking sites, but, in true Gunn style, he obviously thought that the rules didn't apply to him.

Liverpool

Today, reports of street violence and the levels of that violence are shocking society; however, Liverpool has a long history of street gangs and crime dating back to the mid-19th century. This way of life was particularly prevalent during the Victorian era. In the 1800s, there were a number of sectarian or politically motivated gangs who carried out mindless attacks as well as robberies, brutality and violence purely for pleasure. The focus of gangs shifted towards the end of the century, when brewing families began to make a great deal of money from public houses and beer houses. The wealth of these Victorian brewers added to the social and criminal problems of central Liverpool and gave a number of gangs opportunity for violence.

Gangs of men would hang around pubs and beer houses intimidating those passing by to hand over a pint or two. Those who declined could face a beating. The wave was fairly gentle to begin with, but, as the 1880s got under way, violent thugs and gangs increased. Gangs were also beginning to lay claim to "territory" in the city. The Regent Street Gang based itself, unsurprisingly, in Regent Street. There were also religious gangs, often Catholics, who made robbery their specialty. They, too, were extremely territorial. Gangs fought other gangs and there was little consideration for the innocent people that happened to find themselves caught in gang warfare. It was a ruthless, lawless time, when gangs had counterparts in the United States. At a time when Liverpool was the city from which many immigrants left, bound for a new life across the Atlantic, the prejudices and gang warfare went too, with many disaffected youths yearning for a better life. Weapons were used to beat rival gang members about the head and face. The most feared of all the gangs were the dockers who made up the High Rip Gang. These men were highly "sophisticated" in their approach towards victims and didn't just dish out a good beating. They watched and waited, established when their intended victim was paid and then robbed him. It was well-planned, well-executed and organized. The level of violence this gang used showed no mercy and members were more than content to kick a man to death. Child gangs were also prevalent in the city during the Victorian era, and, like today's youth gangs, were often organized and controlled by older criminals. Also like today, these gangs provided a feeling of belonging when there was little else on offer, and many of the gangs consisted of young boys following in the footsteps of their older relatives and peers. While violence was part of child gang culture, much of the crime carried out was connected to house burglaries and robbery. Punishments, however, were almost as cruel as the gangs who operated in the centre of the city. Industrial schools meted out brutal punishments, and discipline was harsh. Incarceration meant living in desperate conditions while serving "time", which also came in the form of training ships. Other punishments included flogging and the death penalty. However, Liverpool gangs continued to flourish through the centuries – and would shift with the changing times just as they did in other cities both in the UK and further afield. In fact, 200 years later, gangs were still showing how brazen they could be.

In August 2007, on a chilling Internet video, a member of the gang suspected of murdering Rhys Jones brandished a pistol. The footage of the young gunman – with just his eyes visible behind his hood – is one of a number of sinister scenes from the two-minute film posted on YouTube. It featured several masked members of the Croxteth Crew showing off a fearsome array of sawn-off shotguns and firearms as they make their swaggering contempt for the law quite clear. The teenage thugs' readiness to use weapons to settle scores with their Strand Gang rival – based in nearby Norris Green – left law-abiding locals cowering in fear. One terrified woman told reporters: "The kids pass guns around to each other as if they were football cards. There is no mystique about guns, there's no fear – they are just a status symbol. Now it seems anyone who wants one can get hold of one." The grainy YouTube clip also showed a close-up of one young gang member wielding a pistol and wearing gloves to stop his fingerprints appearing on it. In another clip, a boy loads a shotgun and menacingly puts his finger on the trigger. The film, set to a hip-hop soundtrack, also features the young gang members crudely showing off their other accessories as they make pit bulls fight one another and race motorbikes down streets. The video disgusted several YouTube users – one wrote after Rhys' murder: "That was scum. Whoever killed that kid should rot in hell." Another seethed: "You should be prosecuted for showing crap like this. If you think this is cool, you will also be street rats like these people."

Towards the end of August 2007, the mum of murdered 11-year-old Rhys Jones made a direct appeal to her son's killer and begged: "Please, turn yourself in." Melanie, 41, sobbed as she asked: "How can you live with yourself? You're not going to be able to live with yourself. It's going to be on your conscience for the rest of your life. Turn yourself in because they are going to find you ..." Speaking at a press conference, Melanie sat alongside her husband, Stephen. Melanie said that she and her husband were shocked to learn the hooded bike-riding killer who shot dead their son in Croxteth Park could have been as young as 13. She said: "It's horrendous. What are their parents doing ...?" Melanie asked at the press conference who these parents were and what they were doing. She also said that the killer's parents must have known what he was up to, or didn't they care, she asked. She described how there were no boundaries any longer and no respect. Stephen stated that he wondered how such a young lad had become a killer. He said: "The thing is that if you take away the gun, you take away the hoodie, you take away the bike, it's just a little boy – a kid." The couple added that they and 17-year-old son Owen planned to leave their three-bedroom home because they could not bear to walk to the shops past the spot where Rhys was gunned down.

Melanie added: "We've lived there 17 years and we've never

had trouble, never been frightened – never knew anything about guns. Yes, there are gangs of kids around, but there's gangs of teenagers everywhere – especially up at the shops where they congregate. Maybe I live in a bubble, but I never thought they went up there with guns." The mother of Rhys Jones described how she no longer felt safe. Melanie and Stephen were speaking as Merseyside Police gave their biggest hint that Rhys' murder was linked to a Croxteth gang war. Officers said he may have been caught in the crossfire in a long-running feud between the 31 members of the Croxteth Crew and the 41 gang members of their rivals, the Strand Gang. Detectives said the ages of the gang members ranged from 16 to 50. Of the 72 gang members that had been in the area at that time, 17 were in custody and two were dead.

Police sources also said they were investigating whether an 18-year-old model who was close to the murder scene could provide vital clues. The girl was in a car at the shopping centre a few yards from the Fir Tree pub car park when Rhys was shot. The killer was said to be similar to a mystery gunman who fired on the girl's home eight months earlier. The girl, who was not named, used to date a well-known gang member, jailed in 2006 for firearms offences. However, it was claimed that she had been at the centre of a feud after falling for a rival gang member. Police denied this, but did admit they had questioned the girl. Police believed that the killer was aged between 13 and 15. They had, at this point, arrested 10 teenagers – six of whom had been bailed and four released without charge. But despite numerous appeals from police, Rhys' parents, community leaders and Everton football stars, potential witnesses failed to come forward. There was a wall of silence surrounding the death of this young boy.

Melanie said at the press conference that she knew people were frightened, but she urged them to do the right thing. She said: "They fear for themselves and for their families. It is the gangs, isn't it? It is the guns. I would be frightened. But witnesses need to come forward. The people who were there need to come forward." Rhys' mum asked witnesses to be brave. She also stated that she believed that the killer's family knew who he was and said that her family were struggling to deal with their grief – but were determined to struggle on until the killer was caught. Melanie said: "We have to be strong. We can't fall apart. Owen is very quiet. He can't even say the words. He can't even say what has happened to his brother. It's going to take him a long time to get over it – if he ever gets over it. I don't think he will. I don't think any of us ever will. You've just got to learn to live with it, if you can."

Meanwhile, other incidents were also making the headlines. Scotland Yard's Operation Trident was investigating the shooting of a woman in her 30s who was left seriously ill in hospital, and a girl, celebrating her GCSE results, who was beaten up as a cheering mob filmed the event on mobiles. Lauren Edmunds, 16, was set upon after innocently agreeing to meet fellow pupils to compare results. However, she was ambushed by a girl who kicked, punched, and banged her head into a wall in front of 20 yelling kids. Lauren did not retaliate, even though she was a kick-boxer. She suffered a broken nose, black eye and bruising. A car nearly hit her after she was pushed in the road in Darlington. The young student said she felt betrayed, lost and empty after the attack. The footage of her ordeal was later given to her by one of the group. It was passed to Durham Police and a girl aged 16 was arrested. In a further incident, a gang wielding metal baseball bats crashed a 16-year-old's birthday celebrations and trashed his parents' home. Five teens, who had earlier been turned away from the party, fetched their "older brothers", who stormed the house. The terrified guests had to lock themselves in upstairs rooms. One boy was badly beaten before the gang was stopped by neighbours. The boys' parents told reporters that the kids were traumatized by the ordeal.

One month later, on 27th September 2007, Rhys Jones' parents paid tribute at their murdered son's graveside on what would have been his 12th birthday. As they did so, it emerged that one youth had been named by 12 people as a prime suspect in his shooting. The family left a blue-and-white football bouquet and said a prayer to Everton fan Rhys. A poignant message on their flowers said: "To Rhys, 12 today. Never out of our thoughts. Love Mum, Dad, Owen. XXX." The family stayed by the grave for 15 minutes before driving back to their home in Croxteth. Mrs Jones said: "It's so quiet at home. It's never going to be the same again." When Rhys was shot, he had been walking home from football practice. At least two youths were named after 40 people rang in, following the heartfelt appeal by Rhys' parents and CCTV images of the suspected killer, which were shown on BBC1's *Crimewatch*. It was believed that both youths had been previously questioned. *Crimewatch* investigators were also told that an adult allegedly connected with drug gangs supplied the gun. One caller gave information about where the weapon might be found. Police, who believed the killer was definitely a teenager, said: "The net is closing. It's only a matter of time." Rhys was believed to be an innocent victim of a war between the two rival Liverpool gangs. On the same day that the young lad would have turned 12, four Croxteth Crew were jailed at Liverpool Crown Court for shooting dead Strand Gang boss, Liam Smith, 19, in a 20-strong ambush. Ryan Lloyd, 20, was jailed for a minimum of 28 years, Thomas Forshaw, 18, for at least 20 years, while a boy of 16 was jailed for at least 18 years. Liam Duffy, 26, got 20 years for manslaughter.

In October 2007, a teenage boy was named on YouTube as the gunman who killed Rhys. He was identified on a comments section attached to sickening video footage of the street gang brandishing guns. One Internet user wrote that Rhys was not deliberately murdered but shot dead by accident, adding: "No one set out that night to kill Rhys." But another YouTube viewer replied: "Who da fuck is no one? It was ... who killed Rhys and everybody knows." Police hunting the hooded gunman had already been given the name by dozens of callers. The young killer named was believed to have been a member of the gang, and was living just a mile from the car park where the young victim was shot. The YouTube video clip was posted by the Broadway Boyz, a gang from the Norris Green area of Liverpool. Also known as the Nogga Dogs, they were fierce rivals of the Croxteth Crew. The four-minute video shows the youngsters pointing guns at the camera. It was thought that the bullet that found Rhys had been meant for a member of the Norris Green gang. By 15th April 2008 the prime suspect in the case was behind bars. The arrest over the murder was one of 12 made as 100 officers, many of them armed, swooped on 10 addresses in co-ordinated dawn raids. Armed police kicked down the door of a semi-detached house at 6am and led away a 17-year-old in handcuffs. It was the third time the teenager – the main suspect – had been arrested since the killing. Police had previously quizzed him about the killing and a separate firearms offence. Drug squad officers had also raided the house earlier in the year, but no one had been arrested at that time.

The youth lived with his mum, younger brother and elder sister in a cul-de-sac just a mile from the murder scene, and the close was sealed off as forensic experts searched the house. Police were inside the house, having broken down the door, for 20 minutes, before they led the youth away. Three males, aged 24, 25 and 16, were also arrested on suspicion of murder. A 16-year-old was held on suspicion of assisting an offender, attempting to pervert justice, and possessing a firearm and ammunition. A man of 49 and a 15-year-old boy were held on suspicion of assisting an offender and attempting to pervert justice, and three women, aged 50, 54 and 21, and a 21-year-old man, were arrested over perverting justice. Two hours later, another 17-year-old was arrested on suspicion of helping an offender. All the arrests were at Croxteth addresses. The carefully planned operation followed months of round-the-clock detective work. Crown Prosecution Service lawyers gave the go-ahead for the dawn swoops after examining files of evidence presented by detectives. Merseyside Chief Constable Bernard Hogan-Howe paid tribute to Rhys' parents, who had been kept informed of developments. Hogan-Howe said: "A lot of painstaking work has gone into this investigation, which continues. The public and Rhys's parents, Melanie and Stephen, have been very supportive throughout and we are grateful for their ongoing confidence in the investigation." Before the dawn raids, police had arrested 20 people over the killing, including 17 on suspicion of murder. Some of those were now being treated as potential witnesses. In February, officers thought they had found the murder weapon. Since Rhys died there had been a spate of fatal shootings in the city. Rhys' parents had bravely made a number of appeals in a bid to catch their son's killer, despite the fact that they just wanted to hide away with their intolerable grief. For the gangs, the killing of an 11-year-old boy just intensified the tensions between them. The Strand Gang from Norris Green and the Croxteth Crew had been pitched against each other since New Year 2004. Danny McDonald, said to be the leader of the Croxteth gang, was shot dead by a masked gunman at this time. The rival gangs used guns to settle their differences from then on. In 2007, there were around 70 tit-for-tat shootings and the violence began to spill over into the smarter neighbourhoods. Croxteth Park was especially vulnerable, sitting in the middle of the gangs' territories. The atmosphere on the day Rhys died was particularly tense.

In court in October 2008, the jury heard how Rhys had wandered into a gunman's line of fire as he allegedly shot at rivals across a pub car park. The gunman fired three shots. One of those hit the little boy in the neck. He died instantly. Dramatic CCTV footage of the youngster's last moments was played to a hushed courtroom. The three-second clip first shows Rhys turning towards a metal container that had just been hit by a bullet. A split second later, he is seen dropping to the ground as the next bullet hits him in the neck. A third bullet thuds into a stone wall. The shocking scenes were too much for Rhys' distraught mother to bear and she fled from the court in tears. The jury were heard to gasp as Rhys' dying moments were played on a large TV screen. Prosecutor Neil Flewitt, QC, claimed that the shots were fired by 18-year-old Sean Mercer, from a Smith & Wesson .455 revolver. The lawyer told the court: "At almost exactly the same time as Rhys Jones walked on to the car park a hooded gunman on a bicycle approached the scene. The gunman fired a total of three shots across the car park ... The gunman is seen standing astride his bicycle with both hands stretched out in front of him as if aiming his gun across the car park in the direction of the container. He then makes three distinct movements as if recoiling from the force of firing his weapon. It is the prosecution case that the defendant, Sean Mercer, was the person that fired that fatal shot. It is the prosecution case that Rhys was the innocent victim of a long-running feud between rival gangs operating in the area."

Sean Mercer had been firing at two rival gang members when he killed Rhys. A 16-year-old witness told the court from behind a screen that she heard three shots as she stood near the Fir Tree pub where Rhys died. Another witness to the shooting told the court how her own home had been shot at by gang members because her former boyfriend, Wayne Brady, 20 – whom Mercer had threatened to "get" – wasn't very popular. However, the 16-year-old witness thought that Mercer had been joking about Brady. Mercer was allegedly a member of the Croxteth Crew, but another gang was mentioned in court to the jury: the Stand Farm Heads, based on the Croxteth Park Estate. One of the witnesses alleged that a member of this gang, David Davies, 19, was the gunman's intended target. Mercer, meanwhile, denied murder. However, he was jailed after being found guilty of the murder of Rhys Jones.

Mercer was convicted after a crucial teenage witness was given immunity from prosecution in return for his evidence. Prosecutors said the testimony of the witness, known as Boy X, was the "tipping point". Boy X, aged 17, was given the murder weapon by Mercer on the night of the killing and told to hide it. When police raided his home in September 2007, they found the murder weapon in the loft. He was granted immunity from the then director of public prosecutions, Sir Ken Macdonald, QC. Within days of his statement to police in April 2008, all seven defendants in the case were in custody. Boy X and his family were then put under police protection.

The judge branded Mercer and his gang "cowards" and mindless criminals. Mr Justice Irwin told Sean Mercer that the gangland culture he gloried in was brutal and stupid and had cruelly claimed the life of an innocent 11-year-old. And he scorned the pathetic attempts by Mercer and his six co-defendants to portray their vendettas against their equally thuggish rivals as some sort of honourable conflict. He said: "You are not soldiers. You have no discipline, no training, no honour. You do not command respect." The judge also said that the gang was "remarkable" only in the danger it posed to others.

Melvin Coy, 25, a welder, called Mercer 50 minutes before the shooting to tell him that rival Strand Gang members were at the Fir Tree in Croxteth. After the shooting, Coy drove the killer to his lock-up on an industrial estate in Kirkby to help him burn his clothes in order to destroy forensic evidence. Coy, a father of two, denied going to the lock-up until mobile phone evidence placed him in the area. He then claimed he went there with Gary Kays to get car parts – but couldn't remember what they got, how long they were there or what they did. He admitted speaking to Mercer before the shooting – contradicting the killer's claim that he had lost his mobile the weekend before. One of only two defendants to give evidence, Coy had boasted to prison warders that he would be cleared. He was not.

James Yates, 20, was a leading Croxteth Crew gang member who featured in the videos posted on YouTube. But his hard-man image crumbled when he broke down in tears after his arrest and confession over his role in what had been a cover-up. He was convicted of possessing the gun that killed Rhys, which he had bought three years before the murder. He had given the gun to Mercer. He had also sickened the courtroom by smirking: "All this fuss over a kid." His parents, Francis and Marie, were charged with trying to pervert justice by destroying their son's mobile SIM card.

Gary Kays, 26, lived a rather more cushy life than the other gang members. He drove a £45,000 Audi Q7 and had a good job in his father's building firm. He lived in the big family home, but still managed to "throw his life away". He gave Mercer the precise location of the gang's rivals and joined Coy in taking Mercer to the lock-up in Kirkby to get rid of evidence. He denied he was part of the gang. He had previous convictions for dangerous driving and possessing cocaine.

The gang members showed callous disregard for the child they killed and Mercer was sentenced to life in jail for Rhys' murder. The cocky killer's face, however, paled when the judge told him he would spend at least 22 years inside before he would be considered for parole. After killing Rhys, as well as enlisting the help of Coy, Kays and Yates, Mercer also involved Nathan Quinn, 18, Dean Kelly, 17, and a 16-year-old boy – named in court only as Boy M for legal reasons. Coy and Kays were jailed for seven years. Yates was found guilty of having the First World War gun that killed Rhys. Quinn was convicted of helping to dispose of the gun and clothing, and Boy M was convicted of helping Mercer by disposing of the gun, clothes and the bike he was riding when he shot Rhys. Kelly was convicted of assisting an offender and having guns. The killer had been doused in petrol to remove all trace of gunshot residue. Although many knew Mercer was responsible, locals were too frightened to come forward to help police. After months of silence, Boy X was given immunity for his statement, which – together with mobile phone information that pinpointed the movements of Mercer and his friends – led to the prosecution of Mercer. Mercer showed no remorse for his crime.

Smoking a spliff just minutes after killing Rhys Jones, Sean Mercer showed his callous disregard for the young boy's life when he and his friends plotted to cover up the murder that shocked the nation. With not an ounce of remorse, the killer devised a cynical plan to cover his tracks while paramedics were still battling in vain to save the 11-year-old. Just a few years earlier, Mercer had been like any other kid in the football-mad city – a boy hoping to follow in the footsteps of local hero Wayne Rooney and become a professional. Yet the young tearaway squandered his talent and took a different path – towards a life of anti-social behaviour, hanging around with the small-time drug dealers, gangs and petty crooks that blight inner-city areas. He left school at 15 with no qualifications and began prowling the streets in a hoodie with the sole purpose of causing trouble by picking on the weak. One former friend said: "From a likeable football-mad kid, Mercer suddenly changed into a nasty piece of work. He was a bully, in and out of school."

A family friend added: "From the age of 13 he was a little horror. He would make his mum's life hell, smashing up the house and calling her all the names under the sun. She could never control him. He would just walk all over her." At school, Mercer displayed a complete lack of respect for authority by abusing teachers. He was a regular in detention. One source called him an "obnoxious piece of work", although never in their worst nightmares had they suspected he could turn into a murderer. Another source said that Mercer had no attractive qualities whatsoever. He'd thrown away his talent for football and all that was left was a teenager set on the road to destruction and, ultimately, murder.

Thousands of hours were spent making sure the case against Mercer was rock solid. When the gang member first appeared before magistrates, the thoroughness of the Merseyside Police case drew impressed gasps from the press and the public. Hi-tech bugging devices had harvested damning evidence, there was a star witness, and the murder weapon had been recovered during the first eight months when no breakthrough had seemed imminent. The initial crime scene search lasted five

15-hour days, with 60 specialist officers wearing out 41 pairs of protective boots as they cut down and examined 800 metres of undergrowth. More than 200 other police scoured Croxteth for clues. "Eureka" moments came with the discovery of the gun, the identification of Boy X as potentially an important witness and finding Mercer's bike. There were 3,000 pages of evidence that resulted eventually in the defence admissions about the gangs. In the end, 190 people were found who were willing to speak out despite threats.

James Yates, who supplied the gun, was given a seven-year sentence. This meant that Yates could have been back on the streets within two years and nine months, once parole and the amount of time he had already spent on remand was taken into consideration. He was sentenced at Liverpool Crown Court on 29th January 2009, along with Quinn and Kelly. Quinn, who was serving five years for having a gun, was given two more for helping Mercer, while Kelly was given four years for having a gun and assisting Mercer. The trio sat in the dock, insolent and ignorant, sneering and spiteful, according to press reports. Despite being accused of involvement in a notorious murder, they did not seem to care. They laughed and joked their way through the trial, refusing to admit their guilt. Even their defence teams were appalled, often ordering them to behave.

In another case, Britain's number one drug dealer, Curtis "Cocky" Warren, faced 14 years in jail in October 2009, having been convicted of a £1 million cannabis plot. Police were searching for the gangster's estimated £300 million fortune. Warren, who was aged 46 at the time, and once featured in the *Sunday Times* Rich List, had salted away the cash during his heyday as Europe's most notorious drug smuggler. The former street dealer from Liverpool was convicted in Jersey of attempting to flood the island with cannabis. He hatched his plot just days after being released from a 10-year stretch. The millionaire drug lord earned his nickname "Cocky" due to his arrogant belief that his wealth and criminal genius made him untouchable. Just weeks after his release from prison, he showed his disdain for police by continuing with a £1 million drug scheme despite knowing undercover detectives were bugging his phone calls. Warren, believed to be Britain's richest criminal, was found guilty of the plot. The ex-bouncer used his street-smart business brain to build a vast drug empire, which put £1 million a week into money-laundering schemes at its peak. At one stage, Warren even featured in the Rich List, claiming he made his fortune as a property developer. In fact, Warren, whose dad was a sailor and mum a shipyard boiler attendant, started his real career as a criminal when he was nine. Because he was so skinny, he was recruited by a local gang to climb through small windows to burgle homes. He dropped out of school at 11 and was soon carrying out muggings and armed robberies on the tough streets of Toxteth in Liverpool. It was while working as a bouncer in the city that Warren got his start in the drug trade, initially as a lowly street dealer. But despite his limited education he had a talent for figures and a photographic memory that was a godsend in an industry where nothing was written down. Detectives who later tried to unravel Warren's crime empire were repeatedly frustrated by the lack of a paper trail because he kept bank account details and contact numbers in his head. This, coupled with a ruthless business sense, saw him rapidly climbing the ranks of Merseyside's underworld.

His skills were supplemented by a sober lifestyle that saw him shunning cigarettes, alcohol or drugs – leaving him with a clear head to run his empire – unlike so many other crime bosses in the 20th century who regularly dabbled in their own merchandise. As the drugs trade exploded in the 1980s, Warren developed international links in Europe and South America. He became a trusted customer of the Colombian cocaine cartels and dealt directly with Turkish heroin producers and cannabis suppliers in Spain. His reputation enabled him to get vast quantities of drugs from his suppliers on credit – allowing him to set up complex deals worth many millions. In 1997, the *Sunday Times* Rich List estimated he was worth £40 million, but his true fortune dwarfed that. The outward signs of the wealth from his property business included a luxury flat in Liverpool's Albert Dock and a country home on the Wirral. By then, he had turned Liverpool into the hub of the British drugs trade. At one stage, couriers were taking £1 million a week to London where it was changed into large-denomination Dutch and German notes. These were then banked in Europe. Warren's investments included two petrol stations in Turkey, and he had 250 properties in the northwest of England. He also owned casinos and clubs in Spain and Turkey. In the 1990s, when the rivalry between Liverpool's drug gangs became increasingly violent, Warren relocated to Holland, buying a 16-room home at Sassenheim.

He used it as a base for his drug operation, which was shifting 500kg of drugs a month. But his notoriety had become so great that Interpol had made him their Target One – Europe's most wanted criminal. And the police were closing in. Warren had already evaded justice in 1993 when he was accused of smuggling 1,000kg of cocaine, worth £250 million, into the UK. The Newcastle Crown Court trial collapsed after it emerged one of his co-plotters was a paid informant for customs officers. But, in 1997, Warren was finally convicted by Dutch police of smuggling 400kg of cocaine, 100kg of heroin, 1,050kg of cannabis and 50kg of Ecstasy. The value of the cocaine alone was £75 million. He was jailed for 13 years. Two years later he was convicted of the manslaughter of a fellow inmate and a further four years were added.

On his release in June 2007, Warren was escorted by armed Dutch police to a ferry. They stayed with him until he walked ashore at Harwich in Essex. He headed straight back to Liverpool. Undercover officers were on his tail. He was followed everywhere he went and his calls were bugged. Police listened in as he made 112 calls while setting up his next big drugs deal. Three weeks after his release Warren arrived at Manchester Airport and paid cash for a plane ticket to Jersey. He had claimed he was visiting a girlfriend on the island. Warren had joked to friends that he was "desperate" for sex after his years locked away, but, when his plane landed, he was met by old mate and fellow Scouser John Welsh, a known drugs dealer. Over the following days, the pair were followed as they travelled round the island laying the foundations of a plan to smuggle £1 million of cannabis into Jersey. Warren described the scheme as "just a little starter", as he began re-establishing himself as Europe's number one drugs baron. He planned to buy 180kg of cannabis in Amsterdam, transport it by car to Normandy then sail it into Jersey. Warren carried on with his plans even though police are convinced he knew his phones were bugged. Welsh later told officers: "I knew my phone was bugged and knew my car was bugged." The scheme collapsed when three co-plotters failed to come up with their share of the cash to pay Dutch dealers. Officers were listening in when the deal was postponed and arrested Warren. A jury in St Helier found him guilty of plotting to smuggle drugs. Welsh, James O'Brien, Jason Woodward, Paul Hunt and Oliver Lucas were also found guilty of similar charges. They were sentenced later. Warren faced a maximum of 14 years. Supergrass Paul Grimes, who infiltrated Warren's empire for Customs and Excise, said the drugs baron was a true menace to society. He added: "Warren has spread death and misery on an industrial scale and that shouldn't be forgotten. He's scum." Warren's ex-partner, Stephen French, said he was obsessed with running his empire – not the money.

French, who now campaigns against gun crime, said: "I once asked him why he just didn't give it all up. He said: 'What am I going to do – sit on the couch and watch daytime telly?'"

Curtis Warren was a polite, personable character – he had to be because it allowed him to operate at the top of a dangerous world. He wasn't like the common drug dealers on the streets of Liverpool, with a reputation for violence. He spoke softly and carried a big stick. He was feared, but Warren built his reputation on being able to deliver. If he said he was going to supply you with a certain drug at a certain quantity and a certain price on a certain day, he would, and he was the best at it. Even his nickname, the Cocky Watchman, was based on how well he operated (as well as believing he was untouchable). It was Liverpool slang for a watchman or a guard who is always on the case – he was very, very sharp. Warren knew everything that was happening within the drugs scene in Britain, even while living in Holland. He had an unbelievable talent for handling dozens of deals at once. He was buying cocaine from the Colombians with invitations from Venezuela. At the same time, he was dealing with the Turks for heroin and the Moroccans for their cannabis. He was also getting amphetamines from the Dutch and Belgians. Warren doesn't speak any foreign languages and yet he managed to successfully negotiate with all these people. On top of that he was dealing with multiple customers in the UK and Ireland and kept it all in his head, refusing to write anything down. It was an astonishing feat and testament to his criminal success. All his contacts had nicknames. In Holland, he would call people the Werewolf, the Vampire or Bigfoot. An obese man he knew was Egg on Legs. But Warren did eventually screw up. When he first moved to Holland he didn't realize phone wiretaps can be used in evidence, unlike in the UK. It led to his 10-year jail sentence. It was also the phones that got him in Jersey. He had used local pay phones to communicate with his contacts, but the police were watching. He was a determined and ruthless career criminal, and even today his name overshadows most big characters in UK crime. Warren was given 13 years on 3rd December 2009 over the Jersey plot. Prosecutor Howard Sharp told the Royal Court in St Helier: "Warren orchestrated this conspiracy. He knew the main co-ordinators in Jersey and Holland. He had the necessary clout to direct them." The terms for the other men involved ranged from five to 12 years. The judge then told the court that the police could begin asset seizure proceedings against Warren.

Despite being sent to prison, Warren's tentacles still stretched around the globe. It was suspected that he was still controlling deals with criminal cartels in Latin America, the Middle East and Spain from his prison cell in 2011. However, he faced a further challenge when it was announced that police were to launch a double assault in the courts on his fortune. Authorities in Jersey were set to haul him before a judge in January 2012 to face a £200 million confiscation order after his conviction in 2009. And, in a second attack, the Serious Organized Crime Agency, in a rare move, asked judges to impose a serious crime prevention (SCP) order in the High Court in London to stop him in his tracks when he is released in 2015. Warren's legal team won an adjournment in the High Court to delay a hearing scheduled for December 2011, so that they could prepare the crime lord's defence. With typical arrogance, Warren told his lawyers to fight the bid on the grounds it breached his "human rights". The SCP order, signed by Alun Milford, the chief crown prosecutor and director of the Serious Organized Crime Agency, sought to restrict Warren's use of communication devices and public phones. It demanded that he never had more than £1,000 in cash, while a financial reporting requirement would deter him from acquisitive crime and give law enforcement authorities the opportunity to investigate any wealth he might come into. A source said: "Warren is almost untouchable. A mobile is vital to him. It's all he needs to operate. There are thousands of mobiles smuggled into the prison system and he has the means to get one." Warren appointed himself chairman and chief operating officer of a global operation to flood Britain with cocaine and heroin. His criminal associates said his business philosophy was simple and effective – drugs are products to buy and sell like oil and gold. He was a meticulous planner whose organization resembled the layers of executives and managers you'd find in a City institution. Paul Grimes, a former gangster who turned supergrass after his son died following a heroin overdose, said: "Warren wanted to be the cock everyone looks up to. He loves the status." Much like the Krays from their respective prison cells, Warren, it was suspected, was handling deals from behind bars. Also, Warren was attacked while in prison in Holland by Turk Cemal Guclu, who was serving 20 years for murder. Warren punched the man to the ground and kicked him in the head four times. Guclu got up but Warren struck him again. He hit his head on the ground and later died. Further trouble was to come in the guise of the Whitney family.

Where gangs are disrupted or "shut down", more spring up in their place. As a family business, the Whitneys were available day and night to customers who came from miles around to snap up their goods. However, far from offering a vital community service, the family and their cohorts were a feared gang of drug dealers who preyed on vulnerable addicts to build a multi-million-pound empire that spread misery through the streets of the city. Their ruthless pursuit of riches that brought them flash cars and exotic holidays was backed up by an assault rifle and a stash of ammunition found by police in one gangster's car in 2011. A key figure of the evil mob's operation was grandmother Carol Whitney, 54, described as the "banker and matriarch", who was found to have 520 heroin wraps hanging from a bush in her garden. In December 2011 she was behind bars along with her 11 drug-peddling relatives and associates, who were all sentenced to between four and nine years for their reign of terror, which came to an end in a series of police raids. These included a dramatic car chase with around £90,000 of heroin being hurled out of the window as the gangster fled officers.

In another example of the gang's ruthless streak, a baby was found perched on top of a stash of drugs and ammo, which was stuffed under the baby's car seat. The gang also sold its wares, which included heroin and coke, outside schools. Whitney's son, Paul, then 33, was the gang's ringleader. Whitney's 57-year-old estranged husband Leslie and daughter Lisa, 31, along with Lisa's boyfriend Wayne Hincks, 28, also played major roles in the drugs ring that plagued areas of Liverpool. Detective Superintendent Tony Doherty of Merseyside Police said: "These people were absolutely ruthless in the way they behaved. These are people who are living on the backs of the most vulnerable in our society. They deal drugs. They deal drugs near schools. They have nice holiday homes, go on exotic holidays all on the back of drugs. I would describe them as parasites."

When police swooped on the car of 53-year-old gang member Mary McCabe, they found an SA80 assault rifle, which had been stolen from an army barracks on Salisbury Plain in 2005, and 1,200 rounds of ammunition. In another raid, mum Emma Mackenzie, 29 – Leslie's partner – tried to hide cocaine wraps in the nappy bag of her baby as she passed the child to her own mother, McCabe. In the car chase through Liverpool, dealer Matthew Mayor, 37, threw 2kg of heroin out the window of his silver Mercedes S320. White clouds of the drug filled the street before the car was blocked in by officers. The gang ran day and night shifts supplying heroin, cocaine and other drugs on the streets of Anfield, Tuebrook and West Derby between 2009 and

2011. Unexplained cash deposits totaling £114,619 passed through Carol's bank account. Despite her role as "the banker", she fraudulently claimed £5,000 every year in invalidity benefit. The gang was finally nailed after an undercover operation, in which police posed as addicts to buy drugs as other officers photographed the exchanges.

Officers then stormed one of the "safe houses" that belonged to member Thomas Dowd, 29, and discovered around £80,000 of drugs. At Carol Whitney's home, 49,000 tablets of "fake" pink Ecstasy – worth £250,000 if sold at clubs – was discovered. Five sets of protective vests and bullets were dug up from a flowerbed in the garden, and a CS gas canister was discovered hidden in the kitchen. Twelve members of the feared gang admitted dealing when they appeared at Liverpool Crown Court for sentencing by Judge John Roberts. Whitney was found guilty. McCabe and Hincks admitted possession of a firearm and ammunition. Leslie Whitney pleaded guilty to having ammo. The other gang members were Michael Waters, 25, Gary Edwards and Michael O'Toole, 33, and Neil Brady, 35. Emma Mackenzie was sentenced, but, having already served time in custody, was released.

In June 2012, the rival Strand Gang was back in the press when police armed with machine guns patrolled a housing estate in Liverpool after a man was shot dead and another was left fighting for his life. Joe Thompson, 32, was killed in the early hours, and a man named locally as Kevin Murray was wounded. Up to nine handgun shots rang out during the attack at about

1am, thought to be by a lone gunman. Police were still looking for a motive, but Thompson was known to be a leading member of the Strand Gang. The area around Norris Green had continued to be the centre of the gang's feud with the Croxteth Crew. One resident confirmed that gang warfare was still rife in the area.

Manchester

Drug dealer Ray Pitt, 20, was shot dead and a teenager wounded as gang warfare erupted in Manchester in December 1995. Pitt, a leading member of the notorious Doddington gang, was hit in the head at point-blank range as he drove away from the West Indian Sports and Social Club in Moss Side. A 17-year-old passenger in Pitt's car was under armed police guard in hospital following the attack. Pitt was involved in a struggle for control of turf vacated by another gang leader, who was in jail at the time of the shooting.

Manchester has a long history of gangs, but the latter half of the first decade of the 21st century saw its fair share of trouble. The early 2000s were no different. In January 2003, a legal secretary was jailed for three years for trying to smuggle £5,000 of drugs hidden in her underwear to a jailed gangland killer she had fallen in love with. Lesley Darbyshire, 22, worked for a law firm whose clients included Thomas Pitt, a Manchester gang boss. She was caught trying to smuggle heroin in her bra, knickers, socks and rucksack, on a visit to Pitt at Whitemoor Prison, Cambridgeshire. Darbyshire had Ecstasy and cannabis in her car outside. The young woman, from Dukinfield, Manchester, wept as she admitted drug offences and was jailed by Cambridge Crown Court. Her lawyers told the court that Pitt was "a highly manipulative and dangerous man".

In 2005, two rival gangs clashed at gunpoint in a busy

hospital in the city. The warring gangs sent staff, patients and visitors fleeing in terror as they fought running battles in wards and along corridors. CCTV cameras caught the gang members, many masked in hoods, balaclavas and bandanas, storming the building as three gang members were being treated there. The gangs used hospital trolleys as battering rams to storm through ward doors. They pulled weapons on one another, including at least two guns and one hammer, jurors heard in May 2005. No shots were fired.

Violence had flared between Manchester's Gooch Close Gang and rivals, the Longsight Crew, as gang members were being cared for in different sections of the city's Royal Infirmary. A Longsight Crew member, aged 26, and a Gooch Close rival, aged 19, had suffered gunshot wounds. Fellow Gooch Close member, Leon Johnson, had been mown down in a hit-and-run attack. Feelings were running high and violence was on the agenda.

Each injured gang member was being visited by relatives and friends when word spread that both drug gangs were in the hospital. Longsight Crew gang members phoned cohorts for backup. Prosecutor Robert Elias said: "The arrival of the second group caused panic among hospital staff and members of the public. Staff, patients and visitors fled for their lives." One medic told police: "Lots of boys arrived from everywhere. They were on mountain bikes in the corridors." The gangs hunted each other down these corridors and in wards, the X-ray department and the fracture clinic, Preston Crown Court heard. One youth later begged a police officer: "Help, they're going to shoot me." Eight gang members admitted affray and two others admitted public order offences after the violence in April 2004. Gooch Close Gang member, Antonio Wint, 18, was given 20 months; Fabio Ricketts, 20, got 30 months; and Faisal Aszal, 19, was given 21 months for affray. The trio also received five-year ASBOs. Five Longsight gang members were jailed later, in early May 2005, in order to keep them apart from their rivals. Warren Laing, 25, received 20 months; Tyrone Gilbert, 21, also got 20 months; Matthew McFarquahar, 18, received 16 months; Rennie Dixon, 26, got 26 months; and Mark Carroll, 20, was given 20 months. Leon Johnson, 27, and Bradley Holland, 18, admitted public order offences. Johnson received three months but walked free because of time already served. Holland was given 100 hours community service. Judge Gilbart, QC, said they had turned the hospital "into a battleground", and added: "This was a disgraceful scene."

Earlier in 2005, in April, police warned that a batch of 300 miniature guns disguised as key fobs was heading to the UK from New Zealand. It was believed that British crime gangs had put in large orders for the tiny "designer" guns, while several unsolved shootings were blamed on the weapons, which cost just £15. The guns are just four inches long and fire .22 or .25 calibre rounds – making them lethal at close range. The gun is cocked by pulling part of the key ring. Two buttons on the sides of the box-shaped fob are pressed to fire it, while a third opens it for reloading. The alert followed an inquest in early April that year into the death of suspected gang member, Fabian Flowers, 19, who accidentally shot himself in the head showing off to friends. A police intelligence expert said: "These guns are a menace and officers' lives are in danger. We've become aware that a large batch is on its way from New Zealand where the guns are known to be made. We're doing our best to intercept them." He added: "While the girlfriends of criminals wear Gucci, the men like to carry guns like this. It's crazy because the firing mechanism is often faulty." Scotland Yard's firearms squad had tested a number of the key-fob guns that had been seized. In an internal memo, the Yard reported that the safety mechanism failed to work every time. One officer said: "If you've got a death wish, then by all means obtain one of these guns." Every police force in Britain was sent an Internet video showing how the guns work. Sixteen key-fob guns were seized by police since the first was recovered in Kent in 2003. Of those, 12 were in Greater Manchester. But police were convinced hundreds more were in circulation. Most of the guns were smuggled into the UK from Bulgaria, Bosnia or Serbia, where similar guns disguised as torches and mobile phones were also for sale. Det Chief Insp Russ Jackson said: "It's clear these types of guns are dangerous and I'm certain there are still some in circulation. If anyone has any information about the whereabouts of more of these guns, then please call the police." Detectives were working with Customs and Excise and the National Criminal Intelligence

Service (as it was called at the time) to stop further shipments entering the country.

Self-inflicted victim Flowers – said to belong to notorious Manchester gang, the Longsight Crew – was fiddling with a fob-gun when he shot himself. Friend Gary Woods, who was with Flowers in the High Society club, in Stockport, told an inquest: "He had something in his hand and was talking about safety. He said: 'I'm going to put it to the test – watch.' He put it to his head and I heard a bang. When it happened it was dead fast. I got the impression he thought the safety catch was on and it was safe." In March 2005, Leon Ellison, 26, also from Manchester, was jailed for five years after firing both barrels of a key-fob gun in a street scuffle in Nottingham. Anyone caught in possession of a deadly key-fob gun faced a minimum five-year prison sentence, said police.

Public places and buildings that should be a quiet sanctuary for people seem to have become bloody battlegrounds for gangs in Manchester. In March 2006, hitmen shot two people in a pub. In a twist, they themselves were executed by other drinkers from the bar before they could reach their getaway car. Witnesses said that two Asian men wearing leather gloves ran into the pub and blasted the men drinking at the bar. As they fled, they were chased and caught about 75 yards away. In what appeared to be a gangland execution, one man was blasted through the back of the head as he knelt down. The other was shot in the back. A witness, too scared to give his name, said: "We were watching the Manchester United–Newcastle game when two Asian-looking guys walked in. They had woolly beanie hats on but suddenly lowered them over their faces and they were really balaclavas.

"They began shooting and shot two lads. They ran out and a group of people ran after them. The gunmen appeared to be rushing to a black Mondeo but they both got shot on wasteland before they could reach it. It was terrifying." A number of children witnessed the horrific shooting. The father of one youngster claimed: "My son was playing football with his pals when the men dashed out of the pub. One was kneeling down and was shot through the back of the head. The other was shot in the back. All the lads were stood around the man who had the back of his head shot off." Paramedics who arrived within minutes found the chased men already dead. They covered the bodies with white sheets. It was believed the shooting, at the Brass Handles pub in Salford, was linked to a turf war between rival gangs from Manchester and Salford. Armed police, shadowed by a force helicopter, flooded the Pendleton area. The two men shot at the bar were rushed to hospital. They were treated at Hope hospital. Supt Leor Giladi, of Greater Manchester police, said: "This horrific incident happened in a packed pub while fans watched football. Two mixed-race men have died and two white men are receiving hospital treatment. Their condition is serious." He added: "Gang warfare has been a problem in the past here but we don't yet know the full motive. We have a large police presence here urging calm among the local community and appeal for any witnesses to come forward."

The double murder came three days after a 37-year-old man was blasted in the neck by two men. He was in a stable condition in North Manchester General Hospital. A motive for the shooting was unknown at the time. Manchester was quickly dubbed "Gunchester" after Moss Side was plagued by Yardie-style drug turf wars, starting in the early 1980s. In 2005, alleged gunrunner Ernest Gifford, 45, was shot at home in the same street as Jessie James. The death of the gangs' youngest victim, Benji Stanley, 14 – shot in January 1993 while queuing for a takeaway – led to a temporary ceasefire.

However, violence peaked in the mid-1990s as the Gooch Close and Pepperhill gangs and the Pitt Bull Crew emerged. In just five years, 27 people died and 250 were injured. Then, in 2001, four Gooch Close leaders were each jailed for nine years after police caught them having a Mafia-style summit. In 2002, 30 Pitt Bull members, including leader Tommy Pitt, were jailed. In March 2005, Carlton Alveranga, 20, and Richard Austin, 19, were shot dead. They were the two mixed-race men who had tried to carry out a hit at the pub in Salford. Police said at the time that 76 per cent of gang members were African-Caribbean or mixed race.

Jessie James, 15, was killed by three bullets in Moss Side. The innocent teenager's heartbroken mother warned in September 2006: "There will be a sea of blood if nothing is done." Barbara Reid added: "People are tired of the bloodbath around here, tired

of the pain that leaves mothers aching and families destroyed."
As police said, Jessie had been in the "wrong" place at the
"wrong" time. Mrs Reid added: "I have always lived in fear here.
I have always wanted to get out of Moss Side and have been
on the housing list for the last two years, but nothing has been
done. I told them I was desperate to get out but they ignored
my plight."

Jessie was shot in the chest and stomach in a Moss Side
park as he rode his bike home from a party. Speaking of her
son's killers, Mrs Reid said: "I do not know how they could stoop
so low as to bring these weapons here. It is a disgrace, it is a
tragedy. I cannot believe it has happened. Jessie was a lively,
bubbly boy who was loved by everyone." His sister Rosemary, 28,
added: "All I feel is emptiness." Detective Supt Tony Cook said:
"We believe Jessie happened to be in the wrong place at the
wrong time. There is not a shred of evidence to suggest he was
a member of any gang or involved in gangs in any way. Jessie's
killers intended to shoot someone and may have mistaken Jessie
for that person." Cook refused to rule out a link to a spate of
shootings in the area in previous weeks. He apologized for the
police's failure to contact Mrs Reid until nine hours after the
killing. Jessie's friends described him as a polite, well-mannered
boy who would never have become involved in Moss Side's
murky underworld. The pals laid flowers at the gates to the park
where Jessie was shot and at his family home nearby. Some of
them broke down as they left messages. One friend said: "He

was innocent and that's why everyone is so devastated. If it was to do with gangs and it was a set-up, then they got the wrong person." Community leaders called on residents to help force out the gun gangs that roam Moss Side. Pastor Michael Simpson, of the Seventh Day Adventist Church, said: "We have got to sort this out", while local MP, Tony Lloyd, said: "We will not let these gunmen rule our streets."

A woman gangster, dubbed the Black Widow, was jailed for life on 8th May 2007 over a bungled "hit" in which two gunmen were killed. Convicted gunrunner Constance Howarth, then aged 38, acted as the "spotter" when Carlton Alveranga, 20, and Richard Austin, 19, shot their target, David Totton, and another man in the pub in Salford. But Alveranga's gun jammed and the hitmen were leapt on by drinkers and disarmed. Manchester Crown Court heard how a gangster in the pub shot both men with their own weapons. Their victims survived, but refused to co-operate with police. Ian McLeod, 42, of Radcliffe, Greater Manchester – leader of the city's Doddington gang in Moss Side and the man who made the two gang members carry out the hit – was jailed for life with a minimum 21 years. Howarth, of Salford, was given a minimum of 20 years. Mr Justice Andrew Smith said: "You are incorrigibly involved in violent crime. You will always present a danger to the public."

In September 2007, fuelled by vodka from plastic cups, two teenage girls howled with laughter as they pointed guns at passers-by in a Manchester street – then brazenly targeted a

CCTV camera. The black pistols were thought to be replicas, but as police tried to identify the pair, one senior officer said their twisted fun could have had horrific consequences. He said: "The standard response would be to deploy armed officers. It wouldn't matter whether the gun was real or a replica – if it was pointed at an officer, it would be treated as a real gun." The girls spent five minutes aiming and cocking the weapons – which looked like 9mm automatics – at a CCTV camera in the city. David Arathoon, owner of CCTV Surveillance Solutions, took the footage. He said: "I saw two girls sat there playing with what looked like guns. I couldn't believe it. They looked to be pointing them at people walking past. After a while, they pulled out some cups and a bottle of vodka. They didn't look more than 16." The release of the images came days after the fatal shooting of Rhys Jones (in Liverpool). Mr Arathoon went on: "I don't know what these girls were playing at. If they had a brother like the lad in Liverpool, I don't think they'd find it so funny." Police in Manchester had fought to rid the city of its 1990s nickname, "Gunchester", and Detective Chief Supt Dave Keller said: "Given the situation nationally and locally with guns, it's highly irresponsible and unfair on victims of gun crime."

Gun crime in the city fell by 12 per cent in 2004/05 and by 4 per cent in 2005/06. The number of people killed in shootings fell from eight to four. In August 2007, there was a series of shootings in the city in which a man of 23 died and several people were hurt, including a teenager. It was not an offence to buy replica firearms, but it was an offence to carry one in a public place without permission. Things began to change: shootings had fallen by 92 per cent in 2009, and the Gooch Gang was back in the press, but not due to its usual activities.

The reason that this notorious gang found its way back into the national press was precisely because of the fall in gun crimes. It had been destroyed. Delighted detectives celebrated in April 2009 after smashing the brutal drug mob that had previously terrorized the city. Eleven members of the Gooch Gang were found guilty of charges ranging from murder and gun possession to drug dealing. Since their arrests, gang-related shootings in Manchester fell by a massive 92 per cent and there were no gang-related murders for a year. Gang leaders Colin Joyce, 29, and Lee Amos, 32, were convicted of the drive-by killing of a mourner at the funeral of a man who had been "executed" months earlier. Joyce, who called himself the General, had left a trail of mayhem across Manchester as his gang tortured and attacked rivals. It culminated in the murders of Ucal Chin, 24, and Tyrone Gilvert, 23, who were linked to the rival Longsight Crew, Liverpool Crown Court heard. Joyce, Amos and nine "foot soldiers" were sentenced on 7th April 2009.

Detective Chief Inspector Stephen Eckersley said: "I am absolutely delighted the members of this ruthless gang are off the streets. They were prepared to use deadly violence to enforce their will and settle scores with rivals. The implications of the conviction for the city are immense." The judge compared

Joyce to Al Capone as he jailed the gang leader for 39 years. Mr Justice Langstaff told Colin Joyce: "You were involved in gang-related activity which is all too reminiscent of Al Capone and Chicago during prohibition." Joyce smirked while he was handed two mandatory life sentences for murder. All 11 members of the Gooch Gang were convicted of 27 charges. In the six-month trial at Liverpool Crown Court, a jury heard how they terrorized Manchester. The judge said: "Manchester is not the Wild West, but many of you treated it as if it were." The remainder of the gang faced sentences ranging from life to five-and-a-half years. However, it didn't end there.

Despite the fact that these cold-blooded killers had gunned down victims, the gangland killers and their families were furious when their mugshots were used in an anti-crime campaign. Relatives of Joyce and Amos said that using the pictures of the thugs on posters breached their human rights. The murderous pair claimed that hostility towards them had grown since the posters – which aimed to steer youngsters in Manchester away from gangs – were released. The former gang leaders said they had not been warned about the campaign, which showed the criminals as they are, and how they might look when they're released as old men. Civil rights group Liberty backed the families. Legal director James Welch said: "This is not about protecting criminals in jail, but safeguarding innocent family members who have done nothing wrong." But Greater Manchester Police Chief Constable Peter Fahy, added: "In this case we were concerned with the ultimate human right ... the right to life, and this far outweighed any privacy rights. We used the posters to let young people, who may be tempted into gang violence, understand the real-life consequences. We still believe it was the right thing to do."

Gangs

Birmingham

A picture of four innocent party girls taken hours before they were gunned down summed up the ugly futility of Britain's gun culture in January 2003. Twins Charlene and Sophia Ellis, 18, and their friend, Letisha Shakespeare and cousin, Cheryl Shaw, both 17, were caught in sub-machine gun crossfire as rival gangs traded more than 30 9mm shots.

Charlene and only child Letisha were killed. Sophia was seriously injured and said to be stable and under armed guard in hospital. Cheryl was shot in the hand and was able to go home fairly soon after the attack. As a huge murder hunt was launched, a cousin of the twins, who did not want to be named in the press, said: "When you look at the picture it really brings it home to you. They were so young and beautiful." The cousin added: "They had their whole lives to look forward to. Now two have been taken from us. It's all so pointless. We're devastated." The girls, described as "good, quiet, churchgoing girls", went out to enjoy a party. "Look what happened to them," said the cousin. "It's very difficult to come to terms with. The twins' mother can hardly speak for grief."

The girls were blasted at about 4am on New Year's Day, a Thursday, after leaving a party in a hairdressing salon at Aston, Birmingham. On 3rd January 2003, police confirmed that the youngsters' only "crime" was to be in the wrong place at the wrong time in a city plagued by a string of shootings likened to gang turf wars. Murder hunt chief, Detective Superintendent Dave Mirfield, said: "These girls weren't members of any gang. They were innocents on a night out with friends. Their families are absolutely traumatized. Whatever condition the gunmen were in they can't help but feel completely ashamed. I urge them to come forward." But despite £10,000 rewards, it seemed witnesses were too terrified to help police inquiries. Mr Mirfield admitted: "It is a sad fact that there is a reluctance by people to come forward, but we need them to do so." Detectives believed there were up to 100 guests at the party. But many had fled by the time officers arrived, leaving only around 30 at the scene. The twins, of Newtown, and their cousin and friend, of Nechells, had posed happily together for a photograph in front of a Christmas tree before leaving for their party. Mr Mirfield was holding the picture when he held a press conference at West Midlands Police HQ in Birmingham. As he spoke, the girls' devastated families were being comforted by police liaison officers. Letisha's mother, Marcia, 36, was too upset to speak. But the teenager's tearful grandmother, Ruby, said: "We don't understand how innocent girls who went out to enjoy themselves can be shot dead. They were so excited. For something so terrible to happen when they were celebrating is just awful. The only person that my daughter could ever talk to was Letisha and now she's gone."

Charlene had battled to overcome leukemia as a child. Her mother, Beverley, was distraught. Elder brother Gary was keeping a hospital vigil over his sister Sophia. Neighbour Huler Henry,

40, said: "I saw the twins on the evening of the party. They were getting ready to go out to enjoy themselves. They were such a happy pair of teenagers. They were inseparable." On 3rd January a wide area around the parade of shops housing the hairdressing salon remained sealed off, with six police standing guard. Detectives, who described the shootings as "exceptional in their brutality", had stepped up armed patrols across the city. The girls died on Birmingham's notorious Birchfield Road, which was the boundary between two of the city's most vicious gangs – the Johnson Crew, from Aston, and the Burger Bar Boys, from Lozells. The gangs had clashed for 10 years by this point, resulting in a string of murders, armed robberies and drive-by shootings. They were thought to have links to other black gangs based in Manchester and London, who dispensed death for motives as casual as treading on someone's toes. The mother of one murder victim appealed for witnesses to help the latest investigation.

Gleenreid Allen's son, Corey, 28, had been shot dead in a Handsworth nightclub two years earlier. She believed the Burger Bar Boys were responsible. Speaking at the scene of the New Year murders, where one tribute read: "This day shall never be forgotten", Mrs Allen said: "These people have absolutely no regard for human life and it has got to stop. Here we have two girls killed senselessly. How can you just go and kill randomly like that? There's a mistrust of the police. But if the community doesn't help the police these gangs will keep on killing again and again." Mothers Against Violence founder, Patsy McKie,

53 – whose son Junior, 20, was shot dead by mistake near his Manchester home in 1999 – said: "I felt sick to my stomach when I heard about those two young girls. Surely now people will stand up and open their eyes to what is really going on. This indiscriminate killing is coming to all our doors. I want people to be braver. If they witness a crime, they should stand up and say so." Commander Alan Brown, head of Scotland Yard's Operation Trident, said: "These are not trained killers. They are immature people with very potent weapons." Firearms offences in England and Wales had risen by 42 per cent over the preceding year. At this time, police were seizing more than 140 guns each month.

It transpired just six days after the killings that the twins, Charlene and Sophia, had brothers in two rival gangs believed to be caught up in a drugs war. The Burger Bar Boys and the Johnson Crew were said to be linked to the shootings. Local gangland figures, who refused to be identified, told the press: "Charlene and Sophia have three brothers and two of them are mixed up in the gang rivalry thing. Gary Ellis is a major player in the Burger Bar Boys, while there is another brother who is with the Johnson Crew. The girls were not gang members. They were innocent bystanders, but you can bet the gunmen knew they were related to Gary. He may have been the real target." Police believed that there had been up to eight armed clashes between the gangs at this point. The girls were mown down outside the Uni-seven salon when bullets were fired from a passing car. As police vowed to catch the killers, guns were involved in at least 15 other incidents across Britain over the New Year weekend. Then home secretary, David Blunkett, announced a new minimum five-year sentence for having an illegal weapon. The then Liberal Democrat Home Affairs spokesman, Simon Hughes, whose Southwark constituency in South London had one of the country's highest rates of gun crime, said boys of 14 and 15 were routinely carrying weapons. Metropolitan Police Commissioner Sir John Sevens said: "This culture of mindless violence, which has partly sprung from the increasing influence of Jamaican and American culture, has to be stopped." Police in Britain dealt with more than 9,000 gun incidents in 2002 (a 20 per cent rise), but officers said the biggest single cause of the relentless rise of gun crime in the early Naughties was the link with cocaine from Jamaica and the escalating trade in crack cocaine. The crack trade was controlled by young black men who carried high-powered automatic pistols. In the 12 months to January 2003 more than 30 young men and women, either black British or Jamaican, had been shot dead, and 250 others wounded on the streets of London, Birmingham, Manchester, Bristol and Nottingham. Police said that one in 10 of the shootings had been caused by "disrespect".

In one incident in late 2002 in London, a man was shot at a party for stepping on another man's new shoes. Meanwhile, West Midlands Chief Constable Paul Scott-Lee appealed for help to catch the Aston killers. He said: "These are just young people shot down while enjoying themselves at a party. It is not a gang member shooting another gang member. I am confident we will catch the killers, but we need people to come forward and tell us what they know." It was believed at this time that Turkish heroin gangs were bringing in automatic weapons which they then sold to gangsters. Organized crime and drug wars in the Pakistani and Indian communities were thought to be behind another 50 shootings across Britain between 2002 and 2003. The guns flooding into the country were becoming increasingly sophisticated and included automatic pistols, and sub-machine guns such as the MAC-10 and Uzi.

The grieving father of Charlene Ellis found his family caught in a terrifying gangland trap on 6th January 2003. Arthur Ellis feared that his fugitive son, Marcus, 23, may have been involved in the shootout with the rival gang. He believed his son knew his daughter's killer. His other son was also, it was revealed, in a rival gang, which was thought to be plotting revenge for Charlene's killing. Meanwhile, Sophia was still lying in hospital after the shooting. Bowed with grief, Arthur Ellis begged his sons to come to their senses. He said: "They are devastated. Only now with their sister dead will they perhaps understand this madness has to stop. They have to open their eyes." He then made a dramatic appeal to Marcus: "Give yourself up, son. I don't know what you've done, but go to the police and tell them what you know." As he did so, officers revealed that a wall of silence erected by witnesses had been breached and information was flooding in. Murder hunt chief Dave Mirfield confirmed that police had been given several names of people that were thought to have been either responsible, or gang members who might have been at the crime scene. Marcus was a member of the Burger Bar Boys. Nathanial, his brother, was a member of the Johnson Crew. It seemed that Gary Ellis was perhaps not involved at this point. Arthur said Marcus was present at the attack in which the girls were cut down. Torn apart by the tragedy, at a time when his family should have able to pull together and comfort each other, the 42-year-old born-again Christian, once jailed for manslaughter, told how his son, Marcus, had disappeared. Arthur believed that the Burger Bar Boys went to the scene in Birchfield Road seeking revenge for the killing of one of their own. He said: "This party was an opportunity because it was in Johnson Crew turf. They went there to kill people, of that I've no doubt. I think there was crossfire and that's when the girls were killed. My daughters were in the wrong place at the wrong time." He believed that one section of the road was sealed off with a gunman so no one could escape from the party. Then another car drove by, spraying bullets from a machine gun. He said: "They knew exactly what they were doing." Arthur feared rivalry between the two gangs would erupt into an all-out turf war. He was aware that the Johnson Crew now wanted revenge for the attack, and he had been warned that they wanted to start shooting the brothers and sisters of all those who took part. Meanwhile, Arthur and other family members prepared to visit Sophia to tell her about the death of her twin sister. He believed that she may have already guessed.

Arthur was told of the shootings in a hysterical phone call from his son Michael. He knew then and there that Charlene was dead. She had been shot in the head, shoulder and arm. Sophia had been hit in the arm and it was thought she could lose one of her thumbs. Both girls, who were committed Christians, had been warned by their father only days before the shooting to be careful when they were out. He was well aware that the gangs didn't care who they hit. Arthur had been convicted of manslaughter when he killed his love rival, Kevin Powell, in 1993. Since that time, he had turned his back on violence and was appalled that his sons had become involved in it. Police were overwhelmed by the information they were beginning to receive about the shootings – some even came from gang members. When Arthur Ellis was interviewed by the *Mirror* he received no money. The newspaper made a donation to the trust fund he set up for his daughter. Meanwhile, gang members were so sickened by the murders of Charlene and Letisha that they gave six names to police.

One of the informers warned, however, that no one would give evidence for fear of being killed themselves. The informer, who knew the Burger Bar Boys were behind the shooting, called the *Mirror* hotline to reveal that the police were fully aware of who was involved. He said: "There have been calls to the police – and I've made one of them. I want an end to this shit." But, he added: "My fear is that the police won't get the evidence to put those responsible away. No one involved is going to speak. If they did, they would be signing their own death warrant. Those not directly involved like myself don't mind speaking to the police. However, there will be a wall of silence when the police want to take statements. This is the reality of the situation. The really heavy gangsters don't give a damn who lives or dies. They want respect in their own community. That's all they're fighting for. That, as well as the gold chains, the fast cars, the drugs and the cash."

Sophia, known to her friends as Sophie, was told of her sister's death by relatives on 7th January 2003; in the meantime, police offered full police protection – including a complete change of identity – to anyone who came forward to give vital evidence. It was then revealed that Marcus Ellis was No. 2 in the gang responsible for his sister's death, and a former friend said that he was "as good as dead", if he wasn't dead already. He said: "The No. 1 guy knows that Marcus knows everything. What would you do? He could blow the lid off the Burgers and probably help solve at least three murders. His only chance is to turn Queen's evidence – if he gets that chance." On the same night as the shootings outside the salon, it was believed that Marcus Ellis and the Burger Boys' boss were at RB's Nightclub in Solihull. Ellis had not been seen since. Police sources confirmed that Ellis was top of their wanted list. The former leader of the gang, S1, Donald Somers, was asked to help solve the murders from behind bars. He had been jailed in 2002 for drug offences, but was approached by police wanting to know if he knew the whereabouts of Marcus Ellis. There had been claims that he had fled to Jamaica. Senior members of his gang claimed that

Marcus knew who pulled the trigger, but did not know the girls were targets, and that he "would rather die" than help police, despite his father's pleas that he give himself up.

However, Marcus did give himself up voluntarily on 14th January 2003, and was arrested on suspicion of the two murders. He was later bailed without charge, pending further inquiries. His solicitor, Errol Robinson, said: "He denies any involvement and hopes that the wild speculation which has surrounded him will now cease."

Letisha Shakespeare was buried on 14th February 2003, on what would have been her 18th birthday. Around 400 mourners attended the funeral of the young girl who died in a hail of bullets alongside one of her best friends. In a moving ceremony, Letisha's aunt, Sandra, spoke fondly of her inquisitive niece whom she described as having a great zest for life. She added: "Letisha will rest in peace knowing there will never be a day when she is not missed." Sophia Ellis arrived at the funeral, held at Park Avenue Church, Northampton, in a wheelchair. She had recently been discharged from hospital. Police were still hunting the gunmen who murdered two of the girls and injured two others, and had had reliable information that one other victim had been hurt also. They believed that this victim did not attend a hospital and was probably treated locally. They had yet to identify the victim. More victims were to come.

In August 2003, a mother of three was hit by a stray bullet in her own home as a fierce gun battle between drug gangs raged outside. Denise Marriott, 34, was shot in the shoulder as she looked out of her kitchen window. After being released from hospital, she said: "I saw a lot of guys shooting at each other. I shouted to my son who was heading towards the gate and that is when I was hit. I am now worried about reprisals." The shoot-out involved the notorious drug gangs the Burger Bar Boys and the Johnson Crew once again. Denise's shocked husband, Dave, 34, said: "I was on the computer when my son came running to tell me mum was covered in blood. It was frightening." Police were hunting three men. A spokesman said: "This was a serious incident in which an innocent person has been hurt."

Meanwhile, DNA from bottles, glasses and cigarette ends was being used to trace witnesses of the crossfire killings of Charlene and Letisha. Those witnesses that had been too scared to come forward were traced by police, who had analysed samples taken from the party. A spokesman said: "We used DNA as never before in Britain. We have found several witnesses and many have made statements." At this point – in October 2003 – eight people had been arrested, with six, including Marcus Ellis, bailed to face further questions. The *Mirror* visited the home of Marcia Shakespeare in October 2003 to talk about the death of her daughter Letisha. Gazing across the breakfast table at the empty chair opposite, Marcia had hot tears of grief and anger in her eyes. All around the silent house pictures of happier times with her teenage daughter gazed down from the walls and she had to avert her glance. There were school photographs showing bright-eyed Letisha's toothy grin aged nine, family snaps marking birthdays, and the poignant, last picture taken of Letisha and her three best friends in front of the Christmas tree that fateful night. The visit happened the same week that police revealed they were confident they could solve the killings, following their painstaking DNA work.

The newspaper had organized an exclusive interview with Marcia, who had agreed to talk about her loss for the first time in the hope that someone might approach the police with information which would bring her nightmare to some sort of end. It was 10 months since the murders and Marcia, understandably, was still trying to make some sense of what had happened that night. Marcia Shakespeare searched for the right words to express her overwhelming sense of loss and, after a while, said: "When Letisha died, a part of me died with her. She was my motivation and my life revolved around trying to make hers better. Now she's gone and I have to face the reality that nothing will bring her back to me.

"More than anything I miss her beautiful smile and her arms around me telling me she loved me. She was a loving, warm child, who was so full of grace, life and laughter. Her death has left a gaping hole in my life. Now my dream is to work hard to make our streets a safer place so children can grow up knowing they can walk away from confrontation." Recalling the moment she learned her beloved daughter had been murdered, Marcia said: "When I first found out I thought it was a dream – I thought it was someone else until I actually saw her body. Then I knew, yes it was Letisha." Pain flitted across Marcia's face and she said: "It's very hard. Every day you get up and you try and live a normal life but your life isn't normal. She was my daughter but she was also my friend. I've had to change a lot of things in her room because the memories were just too painful and I still keep the door closed. A lot of people think because you look normal and you might have a smile on your face that you're coping, but I just try and take it one day at a time."

Letisha, Charlene, Sophia and Cheryl were inseparable, and the foursome had been looking forward to the private party that night. A pirate radio station circulated details and by midnight more than 100 revellers had crammed into the salon. At 4am the girls stepped out for a breath of fresh air, and 12 minutes later were caught in the crossfire. When the gunfire and the screaming stopped two girls lay dead, the other two were seriously injured. Marcia admitted that the wall of silence that met the police was like her daughter dying all over again. She said: "I'm angry that out of all the people who were there and who saw four girls being shot, not one has come forward. They don't realize the effect this has had on me as a mother. They don't realize I have had something very precious taken from me. My mother told me I should have kept Letisha indoors all the time, but she wasn't a prisoner. I had to allow her some freedom but I never thought in a million years it would be at such a high price. I lost my only child and she was a good child. I had to bury my daughter on her 18th birthday. Nobody can imagine how hard that is. Letisha was born on Valentine's Day and that is the day I laid her to rest. For other people it's a special day, a day of joy. But it's a day of heartbreak for me – the only flowers that I will buy will be the ones I get for my daughter to lay down in her memory."

Vibrant and loving, Letisha filled the Shakespeares' immaculate semi-detached house in the Nechells area of Birmingham with laughter, music and friends. Marcia now faced a haunting emptiness. She added: "People say with time the pain heals but to me every day seems like January 2. The pain doesn't get less." Marcia and the other three mothers involved took part in the BBC's *Real Story* documentary (aired in November 2003), appealing for witnesses. They revealed how their lives had been irrevocably changed since the shootings. Sandra Thomas, mother of Cheryl, revealed that her daughter had become withdrawn since the murders. "She doesn't go out anymore. She just goes to college then home or to her friends. This has devastated her life," she said.

Sandra's sister, Beverley Thomas, mother of Sophia and Charlene, revealed: "It's been hard because they were twins. I look at Sophie and I can see the stress in her forehead and the pain in her face." The four college friends, all regular churchgoers, shared a love of R&B music and fashion. The twins had just formed a popular duo, the Bombshell Ladeez, and their songs, ironically, had a strong anti-gun message. Letisha had wanted to become an interior designer.

In November 2004, it was revealed that the girls had been gunned down by a MAC-10 automatic sub-machine gun. "The army call it collateral damage. In the streets of Birmingham we call it murder," said Tim Raggatt, QC, in court on 9th November. The girls were shot by members of a hit squad from the Burger Bar Boys seeking revenge for the killing of a member by a gunman from the rival Johnson Crew, the prosecution claimed. Tim Raggatt said: "Four girls out for an evening, shot down outside a party in what amounted to part of a piece of gangland violence, gang warfare, call it what you like. A reprisal, we say, for another shooting. Girls who were killed because the MAC-10 automatic is difficult to control and was sprayed in a burst of automatic fire, out of control, by someone who had not the slightest regard for who else might be in the way ..." The prosecutor told the court how "murder" lay at the heart of the trial. Leicester Crown Court heard the shooting was a joint enterprise. Inside the red Ford Mondeo from which the shots were fired were four men and three guns. One weapon was the MAC-10, which held 37 bullets, all of which could be discharged in six seconds. Mr Raggatt told the court that the girls were taking a breath of fresh air outside a party at the hairdressing salon, and said: "As [the car] came by the doorway where the crowd was standing, the men in the car opened fire. They opened fire in a burst from the machine gun that tracked along the wall and discharged what I can only describe as a hail of bullets." The dead girls were both hit three times. The Ford Mondeo was later torched in nearby Smethwick.

Michael Gregory, 22, Marcus Ellis, 24, Nathan Martin, 25, Rodrigo Simms, 20, and a 22-year-old who could not be named, all from Birmingham, denied the murders of Charlene Ellis and Letisha Shakespeare and the attempted murders of Sophia Ellis, Cheryl Shaw and Leon Harris, who was in another car. Simms was said to be the "spotter" acting for the four men inside the Ford Mondeo. Jermaine Carty, 24, of Birmingham, denied possessing a firearm with intent to endanger life. An alleged Johnson Crew member, Carty was said by Mr Raggatt to have been flaunting the gun and to have returned fire. Marcus was described in court as a gunman on a mission of "revenge and reprisal" who murdered his own sister and injured his other sister in a botched drive-by shooting. The prosecutor said: "The intention of those who took part was to kill. It may not have been the desired consequence that Letisha and Charlene died or that Sophie and her cousin were injured. The killers may not have desired that result, but the fact they desired to kill someone is almost beyond question." The QC said that although Ellis was half-brother to Charlene and Sophia, they were not close. The siblings shared the same father, Arthur Ellis, but had not spent a great deal of time together. Jermaine Carty was the intended target that night. He had been with a group of men who were standing near the girls outside the party. The QC told the jury that they would hear from gang insiders, who were moved by their disgust to give evidence against the five defendants.

Nathan Martin was alleged to go by the street name of 23. His brother Yohanne, who had the name 13, was killed on 6th

December 2002. The circumstances of his death were said to be a motive for the drive-by killings on 2nd January 2003. Michael Gregory was known as Chunk because of his size, and it was said he had a close association with the Martins. His sister and Yohanne were a couple and had a child together. Marcus Ellis was known as E-man. Firearms residue on clothing at his house came from weapons consistent with two of the guns used in the shooting. The alibis he gave were said to be false by the prosecution. Rodrigo Simms was known as Sunny or SS. His sister, Selina, organized the party in the Uni-seven salon.

In March 2005, David Mirfield told newspaper reporters that he thought the war on Birmingham's urban terrorists was being won. This came as four of the accused men were convicted of murdering innocent girls Charlene and Letisha. The 23-week trial came to an end on 18th March as Ellis, Martin, Gregory and Simms were convicted. Charges against Carty were dropped and he was cleared by the jury. It was also revealed that pop diva Jamelia's stepbrother, Tafarwa Beckford, 22, was cleared in February 2005 of any involvement in the case. Three of the men, Ellis, Simms and Martin, all had previous convictions ranging from attempted robbery to escape from the police. The four men were eventually nailed by the shell cases from the murder weapons that were recovered from the burnt-out Mondeo. Number-plate pictures from motorway cameras showed a car containing Gregory and Martin as they made their way to Northampton to buy the Mondeo. Information from mobile masts matched the same route, and further mobile phone evidence linked the killers. The police praised the witnesses who eventually came forward to help. They were recognized by Mirfield as having been "brave".

The murders of Letisha and Charlene triggered new calls for tighter controls on firearm sales. Anti-gun campaigner and Birmingham MP, Steve McCabe, said: "What would have been resolved through a punch-up is now resolved by someone pulling a gun and shooting it. We are seeing a growth in drive-by shootings and straight contract killings. This would be harder if it was harder for these people to get guns." West Midlands Chief Constable Paul Scott-Lee said: "There isn't a week goes by without my firearms people being confronted by someone waving a gun. The miracle is we haven't had more people or police officers shot."

The end of this tragedy, at least in terms of bringing the perpetrators to justice, was just the beginning of another. Pop queen Jamelia slammed the gangsta gun culture which involved members of her family and saw one brother in jail for murder. Speaking before Ellis and his gang members were convicted, she said: "It's disgusting. You hear about people carrying guns. An argument breaks out and someone gets hit by a stray bullet. When I was young, people had verbal fights." But Jamelia, 24, anti-gun campaigner and ambassador for the Prince's Trust, was caught in a dreadful conflict of love and loyalty. Her half-brother Tumbi "Muscles" Beckford, 21, was serving a life sentence for shooting Daniel Bogle, 19, dead. He was among four men from the Birmingham Burger Bar Boys gang seeking retribution on a rival mob after drugs went missing. He leapt from a car and pumped three shots into Daniel's head – but got the wrong man. Another of Jamelia's stepbrothers, Tafarwa, 22, was cleared of being involved in the case with Ellis and gang members. However, he took part in a gang sex attack on a girl of 13 when he was 14. A third stepbrother Tesrod, 15, was stabbed to death 11 years before, after pulling a knife on a 34-year-old man. Jamelia said: "It's a very weird situation. Family is very important to me. They're my brothers and sisters and I love them all. My brothers haven't been encouraged by their schools or by society. So people get in the wrong areas. But, at the same time, I feel very strongly about the girls dying. It's shocking ..."

Jamelia had been due to go to the same New Year's party as Charlene and Letisha, Sophia and Cheryl, but she stayed home after allegedly receiving a warning. In a further twist, another stepbrother (there are 10 in total), was wanted for questioning in the murder of Daniel Bogle. Don'tey Beckford was being sought by police in March 2005 in connection with the murder for which his brother Tumbi was serving life. It was a bungled raid by the Burger Bar Boys gang and there was a suggestion that Don'tey had been with his brother the night he killed Daniel.

Meanwhile, Marcus Ellis was given 35 years, as were Gregory and Martin. Simms was given 27 years for his role as "spotter". The minimum life terms for the three gangsters were among the highest ever passed in a British court. The judge had exceeded the 30 years given for the 1963 Great Train Robbery, and said that this crime had involved gang warfare played out on the streets of Birmingham. He stated that lethal weapons were used, the intention was to kill, there was a complete indifference to the lives of others and those who were killed were innocent young people. He also said that there hadn't been a shred of remorse shown, and that society could not permit this sort of behaviour to take place without the "gravest retribution".

Further heartache in Birmingham was to come. The mother of a man stabbed to death in the Birmingham race riots wept as she described "the diamond in our family". It was 24th October 2005 and tensions were running high. Isiah Young-Sam, 23, died after he and his brother and two friends were ambushed by 10 or 11 knife-wielding men in three cars. They were walking home from an afternoon at the cinema as the violence erupted in the Lozells area of Birmingham – sparked by rumours that a 14-year-old Jamaican girl had been gang-raped by 19 Asians after she was caught shoplifting. The attack and fatal stabbing had already caused two nights of rioting. The revelation that rival black gangs, linked to the New Year shootings of Charlene and Letisha, had joined forces after the riots fuelled fears of a race war in the area. Police said Isiah and his friends, one of whom was injured, were "totally innocent", and they had not found a motive. Isiah's mother, Murna McLean, said the deeply religious IT consultant read a chapter of the Bible every morning before putting on his suit and tie to go to work for Birmingham city council. Mrs McLean said he died an innocent victim, 200 yards from his home, as he was not streetwise. She said: "He had very good manners in a slightly old-fashioned way. He was gentle and would hold open a door or help someone with their shopping. He was a private person, deeply religious and reserved. He didn't have the lifestyle of a typical black young man in Lozells. He wasn't out on the streets or at parties, he didn't even have a steady girlfriend ..."

Meanwhile, the Burger Bar Boys and the Johnson Crew had united against Asian gangs, according to the local black music website Supatrax. The gangs' bitter rivalry claimed a number of lives, but the website – which helped spread the rape rumour – had brought them together. The website said: "Word outta street is that members from Johnson Crew and Burger Bar have met to call a truce to recent gang warfare and unite against any attacks from the Pakistani community." The website also claimed that Asian gangs were responsible for the amount on heroin on British streets and that they were calling the shots. It seemed that the tolerance between the two communities was about to expire. The shopkeeper at the centre of the rape claims again denied that any attack had ever taken place. He did not want to be named but stated that there was no girl and no rape. He claimed that the rumour had been started by the pirate radio station. The pirate radio DJ who spread the rumours and masterminded street protests outside the man's shop said he regretted Isiah's murder. He said that it hadn't been intended that anything like murder should have happened and claimed that the attack on the young

IT worker had been about people bringing their own agendas into the mix and taking advantage of an already "hostile" situation. One person, who commented on a local Internet chat room, claimed that the rumour had been around for quite a while and that the initial five men involved had risen to 19 after the radio programme got involved.

Two men, aged 19 and 24, were arrested after an 18-year-old was shot dead in Newtown in the early hours of 24th October. It was less than a mile from the church where a riot had begun the previous weekend.

In 2008, a street gang boss who thought he had been "dissed" was jailed for 14 years on 21st April for gunning down a student on campus. Jermaine Carty let loose with a 9mm Glock pistol after doormen threw him out of a students' union gig for troublemaking, breaking his gold neck chain. Aaron Waller, 21 – who was helping security staff at Loughborough University, Leicestershire, was hit three times and left fighting for his life. He told Leicester Crown Court: "We were only doing our job. But he believed he had been 'disrespected' by us.

"I've now lost my mental and physical strength. All I feel is anger at what he did." Carty, no stranger to violence and gang culture, as covered in the murders of Charlene and Letisha and the shootings of Sophia and Cheryl, was convicted of attempted murder. The prosecution said: "He wanted to demonstrate that he was not a man to be trifled with." Carty was already serving seven years for supplying cocaine.

Yardies

In 1988, the then home secretary, Douglas Hurd, ordered a full investigation into a black Mafia known as the Yardies, as police feared they were taking over inner-city crime in Britain. The gangs were believed to have been responsible for two London murders, up to 30 killings in Jamaica and one in New York, plus a further 20 shootings.

The gangs came to Britain in the early 1980s from Jamaica – nicknamed "The Yard" – armed, well-disciplined and brutal, according to newspaper reports. They were deeply involved in drugs, particularly cocaine and cannabis, and were prepared to kill to wipe out rivals and opposition. But the gangs were believed to be split into warring factions, with no controlling body. A Jamaican reggae star was almost hacked to death in London after he claimed to be the Yardies' "Godfather". Witnesses were too scared to give evidence against these violent gangs – it was a familiar story that would remain to the present day. One man who did "squeal", reggae singer Fitzroy Lloyd Johnson, was shot dead two hours after he went to the police.

Fears were so great with regard to these gangs that security was stepped up around the then prime minister, Margaret Thatcher, in 1987 after one Yardie suspect boasted that the IRA had approached him with a contract to murder the premier. It was also announced, in 1988, that a Yardie Squad was to be set up by police to combat the growing menace of violent Jamaican drugs gangs in Britain's inner cities. Scotland Yard was yet to announce the special team at this point, but a meeting of senior detectives was held on 22nd February that same year. Police chiefs feared that the Yardies – a loosely linked group of small-time criminals who had fled from the West Indies about eight years before – could create no-go areas in racially tense, rundown city districts. The gangs were also thought to be responsible for a huge surge in cocaine trafficking, not just in London, but in Birmingham and Bristol as well.

PC Dunne became the victim of a bloody drugs war being waged across the nation's cities in 1993. PC Dunne, described by the local community as "kindly", had got in the way of an evil gang of killers just minutes after they had riddled drug villain William Danso with bullets. On 21st October detectives hunting the murderers were sifting for clues in their files on the Yardies who were smuggling drugs worldwide. One officer said: "If we can find who Danso had fallen out with we will have an idea who murdered PC Dunne." Yardies operated in gangs called posses and had tentacles spread all over the UK, including Cardiff, Manchester and Liverpool, in addition to Bristol, Birmingham and London. The most powerful in the capital were called the "Spanish Town" and the "Spanglers". Many of their members were thought to be connected with four other drug gang murders in South London in 1993. The Yardies were renowned for their flash cars, women, guns and cash. This luxurious lifestyle was paid for by drugs, prostitution, robbery and fraud.

Yardies originally came from Kingston, Jamaica, from slums with names like Dunkirk, Concrete Jungle and Lizard Town. The criminal network began as a loose-knit mob of petty thieves. Then, in the 1970s, they were given guns – by politicians who wanted them to fight on their side in elections. By 1980, Jamaica was on the brink of civil war after 800 people died in bloody election battles. And, by the early 1990s, the island, with a population of 2.4 million, had a violent crime rate per person higher than in South Africa or Northern Ireland. Murders had risen from 195 in 1974 to 629 in 1992. More than 100 police had died in eight years. The former political gangs had given way to powerful international arms and drugs posses. The Yardies were smuggling and distributing cocaine, crack and marijuana across Britain, Canada and the USA. American authorities said that the Yardies had killed eight policemen in the 10 years up to 1992.

Drugs deals were organized by the Yardies on mobile phones, while travelling using false identities, and forged passports enabled them to flood Britain with guns in the six years up to 1993. When drug dealer Chris Bourne was murdered at his Brixton home in May 1993, he was hit by bullets from four different guns. In August that same year, a 13-year-old girl walking home from church was shot through the arm by a stray bullet as two drug gangs blazed away at each other outside a Brixton bar. A drug squad officer said: "We have had several gun battles fought across busy streets of South London. We hear of guns being brandished or fired almost every day. Guns are a status symbol and they are in the hands of the most drug-crazed, ruthless, don't give a damn people this country has ever seen."

On 9th February 1995, Yardie gang member Leroy Smith greeted a 25-year jail sentence by sneering and cruelly taunting the two police officers he blasted in cold blood. The gun-crazy drugs dealer made a mock pistol with two fingers and pretended to fire at victims James Seymour and Simon Carroll. Watching his savage contempt, Old Bailey judge, Richard Lowry, said: "Dreadful crimes must attract dreadful sentences." PC Seymour was shot in the back and PC Carroll in the leg when they tried to question Smith in Brixton. Carroll ended up with one leg shorter than the other after having a thigh bone shattered. Smith, 26, believed to have connections with the Yardies, told his girlfriend after the shooting that it was a pity the "pigs" were only wounded: "I should have got them good and proper." The court heard that Smith, of Wandsworth, blasted the officers after fleeing police custody. He was being transferred by car between Leicester and Brixton jails when he held a knife to a prison officer's throat and escaped. Smith got to America via Holland, but was arrested in the States and returned to Britain. The jury was told that he helped Jamaican drug barons arrange to smuggle cocaine into the country. Smith was convicted of attempting to murder Carroll, wounding Seymour, robbery and firearms offences.

Police forces were put on alert in August 1999 as one of Britain's most dangerous men was freed from jail. The decision to release suspected "cop" killer Gary "Tyson" Nelson midway through a sentence in which he had terrorized warders and inmates alike, shocked officers spearheading the battle against a Yardie crime wave. A senior detective said: "Sentencing is a joke when one of Britain's worst criminals gets eight years and is out in four. Where's the logic in that?" "It's not as if he's reformed," he said. It was only after Radio One DJ Tim Westwood was shot – just one month before – that the true extent of Yardie-related crime in London became apparent. Detectives were, at this time, investigating the 14th Yardie-related killing in seven months, while it was reported that another 30 people had been wounded. Nelson was one of the group's top gangsters.

The *Mirror* obtained a leaked copy of the all-forces bulletin about him. It tells how he was originally arrested for the murders of PC Patrick Dunne and William Danso, who were shot dead in Clapham. He was accused of Danso's killing although charges were later dropped. The murders remained unsolved. The bulletin continued: "He was also found not guilty of the attempted murder of two North London police officers and two further attempted murders one of which is believed to be drug related. His custodial behaviour has been consistently disruptive and he is suspected of involvement in the prison drug scene and bullying. He has also assaulted and made serious threats against staff."

Heavily scarred Nelson went to Jamaica after the 1993 shooting of PC Dunne. When he returned to the UK he was jailed for opening fire on a van with an automatic pistol. Police were worried that he would get together with his Yardie gang members.

A senior officer said: "He hasn't changed. He's threatening to get hold of guns again. He is a grave danger to the public and the police." Scotland Yard was determined to cut off his supplier. Detectives were hunting for the Yardies' underworld armourer. Forensic tests on seized weapons ranging from pistols to Uzi sub-machine guns bore the hallmarks of conversion by the same expert. It had now been 10 years since the Jamaican criminal gangs began flooding Britain with crack cocaine and their trigger-happy gun culture. And it was at least seven years since the Yard had been made fully aware of the deadly prospect of a Yardie crime wave. Det Chief Supt Roy Clark, by then a commander, had made the chilling prediction as he flew back from a fact-finding mission to Jamaica in order to devise tactics to stop bloody gang warfare on Britain's streets. He wrote in his report on 6th July 1993: "Our strategy must be long term if we are to prevent the Jamaican gangs infiltrating and taking a permanent hold in London and spreading elsewhere." His master plan, however, was in all but ruins. In September 1999, the Yard would face unprecedented criticism about the anti-Yardie tactics he first sketched out. The Police Complaints Authority (PCA) would then decide who should be punished for the disastrous use of Yardie supergrasses, who raped, robbed and murdered while on the police payroll. The PCA action followed a scathing report in 1998 by Hampshire Chief Constable Sir John Hoddinott. The newspapers were reporting at the end of the 1990s the lengths that Yardies were prepared to go to in order to achieve their aims. In 1999 the *Mirror* reported: "they use almost unimaginable violence and have a growing control over the lucrative illegal drugs trade ... Their motive is to make money then return [home] to build a house in the Caribbean. Police sources say there is a hard-core of up to 100 suspected Yardie criminals in London. Up to 200 detectives are investigating them at any one time. Yardies are fiercely loyal groups of young men from the same few streets organized in gangs, led by 'dons'." The newspaper continued: "They fight for territory, drugs and guns. But the disorganized state of the thugs, the random motives for shootings and witnesses' fear of reprisals make crimes hard to solve. In Kingston, where the London Yardie gangs have their brutal roots, two reprisal shooting sprees and a gang feud left 21 people dead in just one week. But, if convicted and deported, Yardies can easily return to Britain using false passports."

In 1999, a source on the Hoddinott team revealed inquiries had unearthed "a can of worms" at the Yard. Detectives and immigration officers feared they would be made scapegoats in a "whitewash" operation. They claimed senior officers wanted them to fail because of the political sensitivity of targeting black criminals in Brixton. Those tasked with halting Yardie crime were confused about how best to tackle the job. It had seemed so easy when Clark penned his battle plan and advised: "The Yardies do not conform to our image of organized criminals. They relish enhancing their reputation by public display of violence, use or possession of firearms and involvement in drug dealing. They like people to know the detail of their criminal acts – even the murder they've committed. But therein lies the key. They are capable of being brought down by aggressive and radical use of informants and information." When he wrote that memo, Clark could call on an experienced band of officers who were aware of the horrifying potential of using ruthless gangsters as informants, but, disturbingly, it was a young constable who became vital to the success or failure of the operation.

PC Steve Barker, nicknamed "John Wayne" because of his height and swaggering walk, was pounding the beat in Brixton when he persuaded a leading Yardie to become his informant. Suddenly he was catapulted to the front line of the Yardie war, often finding himself helping several high-risk operations at once. It would have been a hard burden for a seasoned detective, never mind a PC. At that time, Delroy "Epsi" Denton was top informant on the Yardie underworld. Senior detectives found it impossible to ignore his value as a double agent. One officer told Sir John's team: "I was impressed by Denton's knowledge of Jamaican criminals both in Jamaica and in the UK. From intelligence reports received by PC Barker, I'd no doubt he had committed serious offences of violence in Jamaica. But he now appeared to be an isolated figure, attending a brick-laying course at college, with little money but keen to make extra as an informant. I discussed my findings with my line manager and was given the authority to recruit him. Denton had taken advantage of our weak immigration laws. It would have been unprofessional and morally wrong not to have taken advantage of this situation and use him as an informant in order to arrest persons more of a danger to the public than himself."

Unfortunately, Denton's recruitment carried a heavy price tag. Disaster struck when he was arrested and charged with the rape of a 15-year-old schoolgirl. The case was dropped. Then another bombshell came. In a frenzied attack, Denton stabbed a woman to death, slashing her throat 18 times. The Yard's number one informant was described in court as a "sex-fuelled psychopath". More soul-searching followed with the news that Eaton Green, another Yardie informant, had helped to rob 150 party guests in Nottingham at gunpoint. After his trial, it emerged he was a serial killer who had confessed to 12 murders in Jamaica. Meanwhile, one of the Met's most successful Yardie hunters was forced into early retirement. Supt John Jones was still, however, deeply worried about the Yardie explosion. He said of PC Barker: "I hope he doesn't become a fall guy for all this. He was working really hard for at least three different police squads. He is not to blame for the mess. I don't think that nowadays there is the know-how or the experience at the top. Officers are wary of getting involved in black crime because of racial overtones. There is a pussy-footing attitude ..." He continued: "Things went horribly wrong but middle management should take responsibility. Unfortunately, it's the junior ranks who take the risks – and the blame."

Just a few days later, a man died and another was wounded when a gunman opened fire on a car in a suspected Yardie hit.

It was feared to be the latest of more than 20 killings in 1999, in gang feuds linked to drugs and nightclub security in London. Kevin Hector, 27, was hit four times after being followed to a house in Golders Green, North London. The second victim's injuries were reported as not "life-threatening".

Writing in the *Mirror* in 2000, John Stalker reported on Britain's third biggest industry – crime. Organized crime was bringing more money into Britain at the turn of the century than almost anything else. It was estimated that crime generated an estimated £50 billion every year. And, what's more, that figure showed no sign of diminishing. The gains to be made from arms dealing, drugs, racketeering, even murder were staggering. Stalker wrote: "… it never ceases to amaze me just how ignorant we are about the grip organized crime has on this country. Most of us believe that gang crime is something we watch in the movies or confined to impoverished ghettos. You might not even have noticed the latest incident which sums up how lethal this 'trade' has become. A gunman opened fire on people queuing for a London nightclub in the early hours [31st July 2000], injuring nine people, among them a 16-year-old girl. The attack at Chicago's in Peckham and attributed to a Yardie gangster didn't even warrant a mention on the lunchtime news I listened to. Why should it? This sort of thing has become almost commonplace in British cities today. The statistics of organized crime are shocking. But, unpalatable as they may be, we should be aware of them. Fifty murders a year in this country are directly attributable to organized crime.

Hundreds of men, women and even children, are hurt in shootings like the one in Peckham ..." He continued: "Naturally, there's nothing new in organized crime. Who hasn't heard of the Mafia? Who doesn't know of the Krays and their ilk? But, I've watched gangland activity in this country develop over the past 10 years and it's no exaggeration to say I now believe we are in the grip of a situation which is threatening to spiral out of control." Stalker went on to describe the four main groups of organized criminals with whom the police were concerned. These included the London-based family groups – what he described as the modern-day Krays, who controlled the areas in which they lived. He then mentioned the Turkish groups, whom he described as being responsible for 90 per cent of the heroin imported into the UK. The third group consisted of the Chinese "Snakehead" gangs, renowned for their involvement in smuggling – particularly people – but the fourth group he discussed were the Yardies, which he found "most worrying". Stalker claimed that the Yardies had been around during the 1990s, but that their activities in Britain had "exploded" from about 1995. He wrote: "The Yardies have the crack cocaine market largely sewn up. That is their raison d'être, but to support this they work in racketeering, protection and the gun trade. And they are the group we most need to worry about. The other organized gangs may commit horrendous acts, but tend to fight amongst themselves. To put it bluntly, most members of the public aren't likely to become caught up in their activities. The Yardies operate under different rules. Their activities aren't contained and their victims are as likely to be innocent members of the public as they are to be gang rivals ... Peckham was typical of what the Yardies are capable of.

"They opened fire on people queuing for a nightclub. Innocent bystanders were injured. This could have been a revenge attack – but it is more likely to have been a protection issue, designed to provoke fear and respect from the community. In this regard they are mimicking the American gangs who wrecked such havoc in the Eighties and early Nineties. One of the most notorious gangs in New York was called the Shower Posse because they used to shower people with bullets – not caring who was caught up in the violence. That sort of violence is now happening here – and it is something we should all be deeply concerned about. In fact, many of the crimes being committed on our streets are being perpetrated by gang members who perfected their art in places like The Bronx and Harlem in the United States."

In 1995, the then mayor of New York, Rudolph Giuliani, introduced the Zero Tolerance campaign, hoping to rid his city of these violent gangs. It was successful, but one side effect, according to Stalker, was that the criminals driven out of New York came to London to work. In 2000, it was known that as least a dozen of America's most wanted gang members were operating in London under false identities. In the same year, Scotland Yard believed that some 200 top-level Jamaican criminals were operating in cities across the UK.

Gangster Olatunde Adetoro was jailed in July 2000 after a

crazed gun rampage through Lancashire and Greater Manchester. He had tried to shoot his way out of police custody with an AK-47 assault rifle, and snatched an innocent passer-by as hostage. Other Yardies – Charles Brackett, Mervin Benjamin and Maxwell Bogel – were all fugitives from the FBI. They had all made several visits to Britain. Stalker commented that police forces were slowly getting to grips with the problem, but stated it was notoriously difficult. The "wall of silence" they were met with time and time again hampered investigations. However, one of the most significant developments at the beginning of the 21st century was the setting up of Operation Trident, the intelligence-gathering operation aimed at concentrating on blacks shooting blacks. It was created after the number of shootings in the capital rocketed, largely as a result of feuding between rival West Indian gangs. At one stage, every Yardie incident was handled separately. After Operation Trident came into existence, it provided a central bureau looking at organized crime. Pooled information was coming from MI5 and police forces nationwide. However, Stalker claimed that this wasn't enough and that an FBI-type organization was necessary to bring together all the agencies in order to fight organized crime.

In May 2002, a gang leader feared as untouchable because he had the voodoo power of "ju ju" was finally locked up. Yardie Mark Lambie got 12 years for kidnap and torture, and saw three henchmen go to prison with him. Lambie was number one on the wanted list of Operation Trident. The man, who at 14 was charged with the Broadwater Farm murder of PC Keith Blakelock, was suspected by police of being behind 14 gangland killings. Dept Insp Peter Lansdown said: "Lambie has been thought to have magical powers. There are those that have thought he is a devil, he could not be harmed, and he heals up if he is wounded. Some in his community say he has got the 'ju ju' – that his father bought him this supernatural protection. Lambie's sentence has destroyed the myth of his invincibility."

Lambie headed the TMD gang – Tottenham Man Dem – which terrorized black communities across the capital. Fellow crime boss, Anthony Bourne, 21, who ran the Firm, also got 12 years at the Old Bailey. Warren Leader, 21, was given 11 years, and Francis Osei-Appiah, also 21, got nine years. Lambie, 31, and Bourne, were convicted of kidnap and blackmail offences after an 11-week trial. Bourne was cleared of attempted murder. Judge Martin Stephens said the four were "violent men who appear to consider themselves above the law". The kidnap victims were held in a flat on the same Tottenham estate where PC Blakelock was hacked to death in 1985. That charge against Lambie was dropped and he got community service for throwing petrol bombs. Snatched Twaine Morris, 24, and Gregory Smith, 22, were drug dealers with access to cash that their captors wanted, the court was told. They were tortured with a hammer and electric iron. Boiling water was poured on their genitals. Morris told the court Lambie was known as the "Obeah-man" – a Jamaican voodoo spirit who walks in darkness. Police said the pair felt they would die whether they gave evidence or not. Lambie had also been accused in the past of a club shooting, but the victim had withdrawn his allegation and then had to pay the Yardie £10,000 for the time Lambie had spent in jail on remand. A year later, Lambie escaped unscathed – although one diner was paralyzed – when bullets were sprayed at a London restaurant. Speaking of Lambie's conviction, Det Supt Barry Phillips said: "This is a tremendous day for the black communities, as well as the police."

In Bristol, in 2003, six Yardies were hanging out by a café for two hours, feeding a steady stream of customers with packages passed in awkward handshakes. None of them paid any attention to the police squad car that cruised past, going slowly to negotiate parked cars and a bin liner of rubbish that had spilled out over Grosvenor Road. "The air was thick with the smell of the crack cocaine; aromatic, sweet and metallic."

This description was given by a journalist writing about one of the most notorious neighbourhoods in Britain, a place where crack dealers don't even bother to hide their activities. As the journalist walked along, Dianne, an addict, sauntered over to him. "Blimey, you're brave," she said. "You don't get many white blokes walking around here. This lot think they might be coppers." David Edwards is on the front line: a place found in the heart of Bristol. Drug dealing in the city is nothing out of the ordinary, and the Black and White Café stands out as the most blatant hard-drugs den in Britain (at least in 2003). It was here that a drugs raid sparked the city's 1980s riots, and here that a drugs raid in January 2003 led to 17 arrests and the seizure of 160 wraps of crack. In 2003, the Black and White had been raided more times than any other premises in the UK. The level of dealing there at that time reached such proportions that locals called it the Hypermarket. Users travelled here from all over the South West to score. But it wasn't just the residents of St Paul's who were suffering from the out-of-control drugs crime wave. With 80 per cent of crime in Britain being drug-related, the shootings and gang warfare had repercussions that spread from this area to the rest of Bristol. People like Maureen Gilboy, who lived further down Grosvenor Road, had become innocent victims. Maureen suffered a fractured skull, face and neck injuries, and was partially blinded when four men stole the wedding ring given to her by her late husband. Mum-of-two Maureen was walking through a park when she was repeatedly punched and kicked to the ground. The 49-year-old was so badly beaten that her four-month-old granddaughter was too scared to look at her. Another victim was James Trent, who was bundled into the back of a car in nearby Clifton and forced at knifepoint to withdraw £200 from a cash machine. The 24-year-old web designer said: "I knew they were drug addicts, desperate for cash. One of them had a mad look in his eye and said he'd stab me if I didn't do as I was told." And college lecturer Sam Wild, 32, was another name logged on a crime computer at the local police station. Her £500 bicycle was stolen in the middle of the night from the top of a barge she was renting. She said: "What makes me really sad though is that some kids, probably addicted to drugs, took it and flogged it for a £10 bag of drugs."

In 2003, nobody knew how much crack was being sold in St Paul's but police estimated that every year the city's 200 prostitutes alone spent £11.4 million. It was at this point that Edwards decided to investigate the area. He wrote: "It's 7.35pm on Wilder Street and already three youths standing outside the pub are doing a brisk trade. If you think the average crack user is poor and down on their luck, think again. Most of the customers here are well-dressed and drive smart new cars. A Y-reg Vauxhall Vectra parks up prompting one of the men to approach and lean through the window. Another man dressed in a red bomber jacket saunters over, pulls something from his pocket and tosses it to the driver. Further along in Clifton Place, one of Britain's most notorious set of phone boxes is living up to its reputation. Fifteen minutes after we arrive, a customer stumbles down Stapleton Road – a star tattoo on his neck – unfocused eyes bulging from his head. He walks into one of the phone booths, punches in a number, speaks for just a minute, then hangs up and walks around the corner of a nearby toilet block to wait. Twenty minutes later, a young man on a bicycle pulls up, circling twice as he looks for his customer. After making contact, the pair walk off together before something is passed between them in an awkward handshake. Both then leave.

"Later, a black Mercedes slows to a halt in Pennywell Road

and a huge man – perhaps 7ft tall – gets out and chats to three men nearby. He reaches into a back pocket, pulls out a wad of notes and peels three of them off. He passes them to one of the men dressed in a blue hooded top. Six minutes later, the man gets back into his car and roars off. At 11.33pm, a party in Drummond Road is just starting in a crack house at the end of an alleyway guarded by three men who stare at me as I walk past. Music pumps out through the walls, making the paving slabs under my feet vibrate. Now that it's dark, the dealing has become even more blatant. A white man, in his 20s, wearing a filthy checked shirt, jokes with one of the Yardies before being handed a small package. An hour or so later, I make the mistake of walking up Drummond Road again.

"This time, the man on guard has changed and sits on the bonnet of a Mini Metro, a beanie hat and baseball cap on his head. 'Hey you,' he calls out to me. 'What do you want walking up and down here? Why you been staring at me?' I'm about to turn and leave when his friend springs to his feet to stand between us. 'Hey, he's OK, don't be so jumpy. He was just walking past.' But the other one keeps staring at me straight in the eye until a red Mitsubishi sports car pulls up and an immaculately dressed man steps out. Instantly, the dealer forgets all about me and rushes to greet him. A little later in Ashley Parade, I see a girl called Leanne leaning against the side of a warehouse where she has waited 20 minutes for her first customer. The man in the silver Peugeot 206 takes no notice of the police sign announcing that car licence plates are being logged. Instead, he pulls up and after a brief chat Leanne jumps in the car and is driven off – before returning 10 minutes later. Leanne, who tells me she's just been released from prison, says she charges £30 for oral sex – which she'll only perform with a condom. Full sex is £40 with a condom, £50 without. 'Why do I do this?' she laughs. 'Why do you think? I can earn £350 on a good night and it pays for the drugs.'

"At 2.50am, things are getting busy at the Black and White. There's no sign advertising the café, but you can tell where it is from the lookouts standing either side. As I talk to Dianne, one of the men waiting for trade swaggers over to a silver Montego which has pulled up. 'You wanna buy some more?' 'No, you still haven't given me anything for that phone I brought in. Where's my money?'

"It's here that the most brutal wars to control the St Paul's drug trade have been fought. Originally the Aggi Cru controlled the market, but when six members were jailed in 1998, the Hype Cru stepped in. When the gang members got out in January [2003], they armed themselves with guns and allegedly stormed into the café demanding the newcomers paid a tax. But police intervened before the inevitable bloodbath could take place. Now the café is earmarked for closure, but owner Bertram Wilks – who didn't want to talk to us – says closure won't tackle the problem."

As Edwards left, a blue Peugeot 405 parked up – a white man and woman in the front. She got out, ran into the café before swiftly emerging, something gripped in her hands. Edwards said: "Before the Yardies moved in, the drug choice for Bristol's prostitutes was heroin." He continued: "... dealers started selling 'party packs', containing smack and two free rocks". He estimated that the city's prostitutes, at the time of his surveillance, were spending around £1,100 a week each on crack. At 7.30pm the following evening, having watched and waited for 24 hours, Edwards stated that the whole circle, which carried on all night and all day, was about to be repeated. Two days after Edwards' visit, police arrested a man who was spotted brandishing a handgun as he walked into the Black and White. He was charged with possessing a firearm and immigration offences. Just under a mile away from the scenes that Edwards witnessed, Detective Chief Inspector Chris Smart sat in a building in Avon Street, co-ordinating Operation Atrium. The two-year operation – started in 2001 – had, by 2003, led to 974 people being charged and the seizure of 15kg of drugs, half of it crack, with a street value of £250,000. He said: "We have been very successful in the number of dealers arrested but because there's such a demand for drugs, if we go in and arrest six, 10, 12 dealers, there will be others." Since the operation began, police had discovered that crack was brought into the UK by mules from Jamaica, who were paid £2,000 to swallow the drug and bring it via Gatwick or Heathrow.

It was a similar story just a year later in Nottingham, when it was reported that ruthless drug barons were behind the surge in gun crime in the city, according to police. Jamaican Yardies – many of whom had defied repeated deportation bids – played a key role in the area's crack and heroin trade. In 2003, Nottinghamshire saw more than one shooting a week on average. In the period 2002–03, its 2,435 officers handled 161,404 crimes. Merseyside had just 1 per cent more offences but almost twice as many police. Notts police chief, Steve Green, said his force was overwhelmed.

Biker Gangs

Various biker gangs have been linked to crime. The most famous is the Hell's Angels, which started in California in 1948. The US Department of Justice says it has links to drug dealing, extortion and prostitution. The Outlaws was formed in the United States in 1935. Members were jailed for a 30-strong brawl at Birmingham Airport in 2008. The Australian-based Comancheros – named after a John Wayne film – have been involved in deadly feuds with Hell's Angels. Also in Australia, the Rebels demand members ride Harley-Davidsons. Police raids found drugs, guns and a crocodile. Rock Machine started in Quebec and is active in the Canadian drug trade. California's Mongols attracts ex-soldiers. Another gang from the United States is Vagos – whose members wear green.

The earliest report in the *Mirror* related to biker gangs came in 1967. A pretty teenage girl disobeyed the rules of the Outlaws and, in punishment, had her hands nailed to a tree by two gang members in a "crucified" pose. The gang had "such a hold over her", reports the paper, that "she submitted to the punishment without a struggle". County Sheriff William Heidtman said at Palm Beach, Florida, in November that year: "She apparently just stood there when they told her to, and they just nailed her hands to a tree. We might even use the term crucifixion, although she wasn't hung off the ground." He added: "These girl club members seem to follow blindly any direction from the men."

The girl, 18-year-old Christine Deese, was taken to hospital by gang members following the attack. She told doctors that she accidently pierced a hole in each hand by tripping and falling on a plank which had two nails sticking up through it. Later, she told detectives that she had been nailed to a tree because she refused an order to hand over $10 (at the time worth about £3.50) to one of the gang members. Two 25-year-old Outlaw gang members, "Fat Frank" Link and Norman "Spider" Risinger, were charged with assaulting the girl, who suffered no permanent injury from the nails.

In 1971, five were killed as Hell's Angels battled it out with a rival gang. In the pitched battle, reported Brian Hitchen in New York, about 230 "thugs" were involved in the fight which raged for more than an hour in a crowded exhibition hall. The gangs used knives, guns, chains and clubs against their rivals at a bike trade show in Cleveland, Ohio, in the United States. Five hundred people scattered as the attackers swarmed over exhibition stands. Twenty-two men were seriously injured and 73 people were arrested. The fight started because the Hell's Angels gang, the Violators from New York, had sworn revenge after one of their gang members had been beaten up by an Ohio gang called the Strong Breed. Then, in September 1971, David Bamford – who had been proud of his position as president of the Hell's Angels "Outcasts" – was branded as "leader of the thugs" by the chairman at Ruthin Quarter Sessions in North Wales, after he heard how Bamford's biker gang had terrorized seaside resorts.

Bamford, 18, of Colwyn Bay, was in court as a result of an attack on ambulance driver, Edward Evans. Mr David Lloyd Jones, prosecuting, said that when one of the motorcyclists crashed, someone called for an ambulance. However, when 64-year-old Evans drove to the scene, he couldn't find the victim. Edward Evans then went to a car park where Hell's Angels members were congregating, but they told him he wasn't needed. Lloyd Jones told the court: "When he went to radio for assistance, Bamford quite deliberately broke one of the driver's fingers." Bamford, who admitted grievous and actual bodily harm, theft and threatening behaviour, was sent to borstal. Then, in January 1975, Hell's Angels were back in the news: this time it was a group from London.

A "terror" gang of Hell's Angels went on the rampage through a quiet seaside resort. One man was burnt by a petrol bomb, and another had his skull fractured by a spanner. The gang, the London Road Rats, had ridden from the capital to Barry, Glamorgan, to cause trouble. At Cardiff Crown Court, John Connelly, 22, from Surbiton was jailed for five years for causing grievous bodily harm. Raymond Lovatt, 25, also from Surbiton, was jailed for four years, while Michael Mulkerrins, 19, was jailed for three years. Paul Rogers, 25, of Clerkenwell, was given two years. Each man was charged and convicted of affray.

In April 1979, Hell's Angels boss Dick Sharman was fighting for his life in hospital. Sharman and four of his men were wounded in a dawn ambush in the New Forest. They were the victims of a power struggle between rival biker gangs. On 15th April, an ally of the battered Angels vowed revenge. He warned: "We lost this round, but the other lot are running scared. Now it's war." Sharman, a 31-year-old father of three, was president of the Hell's Angels at Windsor. He and 14 other Windsor Angels were asleep in a clearing at Ivy Wood, near Brockenhurst, when a rival gang charged in wielding shotguns, pistols, axes and chains. Sharman, shot in the spine and pelvis, was in hospital in Southampton and said to be "poorly". Another victim, 24-year-old Edward Jessop, had a fractured skull but his condition was said to be "satisfactory". At her home in Feltham, Sharman's wife, Dorothy, said: "The feud is about whether the Angels should be one national chapter or split into local ones."

The avengers struck at dawn in a peaceful New Forest glade. There were 30 of them, all hell-bent on bloodshed. Within two minutes, they had shot, axed and clubbed the rival group made up of 15 Hell's Angels. Then they simply melted away. One of the attacked group said later: "We didn't have a chance. All we had was our fists. They left five of my mates lying on the ground. One had taken both barrels of a shotgun in his belly. Another had been shot in the spine and couldn't move his legs." The victims had travelled by car and bikes to spend Easter in the New Forest. What they did not know was that they were being stalked by a gang they had refused to team up with – armed men who had sworn revenge. The Windsor Angels arrived at Ivy Wood in Hampshire at about 11.30pm on Saturday night. The area was still festooned with banners and bunting following a visit by the queen the week before. The Angels joined other campers in the forest. A man who made an overnight stop with his family described the peaceful scene: "There was no noise or trouble. I had my wife and daughter with me and if the Angels had been anything other than well behaved we would have left quickly. Then, at first light, a second group arrived in about six old cars and there was pandemonium. I heard bangs, thuds and yells. After about two minutes it all went very quiet." The attack took the Windsor group completely by surprise. They were thought to have been betrayed by a young biker – invited back to their camp for drinks. At 4am, while his hosts slept, the stranger slipped out of the camp. The suspicion is that he went to give news of the Windsor encampment to the rival gang. At dawn, the 30 avengers crept up on the camp. They smashed the enemy's car windows with axes and pickaxe handles. Then they handed out the brutal beating. Nearby, another young Angel groaned on the ground, an axe embedded in his forehead. A Windsor Hell's Angel said: "I got the shock of my life when I saw one of them point a shotgun at my guts. I knew he was going to use it, so I jumped up and legged it. As I ran, weaving, he fired and I heard the pellets zip by me. Behind me, I could hear shots and screams. There was nothing we could do. They were tooled up with everything from axes to shooters. There were at least two pistols. Suddenly it all went quiet and I went back to the clearing. It was unbelievable. The other mob had gone and five of my mates were lying on the ground." Police, many of them armed, set up roadblocks, but the raiders were thought to have mingled with the thousands of tourists in the area. One of the vanquished Angels, nursing bruises inflicted with a pickaxe handle, said: "They could never beat us in a fair fight." He added grimly: "We didn't recognize any of them, but we'll find them."

The wives of the Hell's Angels from Windsor were gripped by fear following the attack. They were terrified that they could become targets in fresh violence. One of them, 24-year-old Marian Jessop, went into hiding with her two children. Her husband Ted had had his skull fractured when he was at the ambushed camp. As Marian packed her bags at her home in Buckinghamshire, she said: "The people responsible for that sort of attack are capable of anything. I'm scared stiff, and I'm not prepared to put my kids at risk. There are bound to be reprisals." Mother-of-two Dawn Barnard said: "I'm terrified every time my husband goes out." Her husband, Paul, was shot in the back during the battle and was rushed to intensive care. At the couple's home in Slough, Dawn said: "I know there will be more violence." Police were out in force as hundreds of Angels roared into the New Forest area. Four young men picked up by police a few hours after the attack were still helping police with their inquiries two days after the battle. In March 1980, 17 Hell's Angels stood convicted over the New Forest clash the year before. One of them, 25-year-old Kenneth Littlefield, was found guilty of trying to murder the rival Hell's Angels' chief. The jury at Winchester Crown Court took five days to reach its final verdict in the trial of 22 Hell's Angels. Littlefield, from Camberley in Surrey, was found guilty of attempting to murder Dick Sharman.

Three years later, in September 1983, police warned Hell's Angels: "Keep your cool, we don't want an all-out war." Detectives feared gangs would launch revenge attacks after a weekend axe-and-knife battle at a party at Cookham in Berkshire. Two men died in the fighting between rival Angels' chapters. Colin Hunting, 34, a father of three from Mitcham, and Michael Harrison, 27, from Hastings in Sussex, were both killed in the battle. Detectives were questioning 52 Hell's Angels, including several women. They believed that the breakaway Windsor branch of the Angels might have organized the party to lure other chapters into a trap. One year later, seven people were shot dead in September 1984 in Australia, when two biker gangs battled in a pub car park crowded with families.

One of the dead was a 14-year-old girl selling raffle tickets for a Father's Day barbecue in the car park. At least 20 people were wounded, four seriously, as the gangs – the Comancheros and the Banditos – fought with pump-action shotguns, .22 rifles, machetes, kitchen knives and baseball bats. The 100 bikers called a brief truce until the car park was cleared of bleeding bodies – then started all over again. The fighting even continued in a local hospital casualty department where the wounded had been carried. Visiting members of the British Motorcycle Club were holding a social at the pub in Sydney when the Comancheros and the Banditos rolled up. A witness said: "There was just a sudden burst of gunfire, and all hell broke loose. Bodies fell to the ground. There was blood everywhere. After the initial gunfire there was bitter hand-to-hand fighting. Terrified parents picked up children and threw them under cars for safety."

Also in 1984, actress Sylvia Syms learned that her son Ben had been cleared of taking part in the vicious Hell's Angel battle in which two men died. For more than a year, Sylvia had lived under the shadow of the trial faced by 22-year-old Ben. Her husband confirmed that the actress had been in tears when their son was arrested and detained in jail. Ben and fellow biker gang members were accused of riotous assembly and assault after the Hell's Angels party at Cookham turned into a bloody battle between two rival gangs, the Road Rats and the Satan's Slaves. A dozen men were wounded in the two-hour battle, sparked off when a girl was staked out, stripped and sexually assaulted. The nine-week trial ended at Winchester Crown Court on 5th December 1984. Twelve men were convicted of various offences, but four others, including Ben, were cleared of all charges. Ben had told his father, Alan Edney, that all he had done was ferry the injured to hospital.

Then, in 1986, a Hell's Angel was shot dead in May in a deadly feud between rival gangs. He was taken to hospital, with a shotgun wound in his chest, by three other Angels, but died as doctors gave him emergency treatment. The victim was named as Steven Brookes, 29, of Fen End, Warwickshire. A police spokesman said: "We believe he received his fatal wound only a short time before he was driven to hospital in Northampton. We are interviewing the three men who took him there." Detectives thought that the murder was the latest move in a bitter territorial war between two gangs known as the Pagans and the Rat-Ae. Four nights before, the Pagans' barricaded HQ at Leamington Spa was petrol-bombed. Neighbours saw three leather-jacketed bikers leap for their lives from the windows as flames swept through the house. Stephen was among them. A pitched battle with knives and clubs then followed in the street outside. Police who moved in rounded up Hell's Angels from as far afield as Humberside and Norfolk. Some were caught after high-speed chases. One was arrested in hospital at nearby Rugby, where he went for treatment for his injuries. The murder squad detectives then travelled from Northampton to Leamington to question them and try to establish if the gang war was the key to the shooting.

In another incident, Gerry Tobin, 35, was shot dead as he rode his bike on the M40. The leather-clad man was hit in the back of the head by a shot allegedly fired from a vehicle that overtook him. Witness Paul Roberts told how other drivers screeched to a halt as they spotted the biker lying face down. He said: "One lady in a BMW took a first aid kit to the man who was lying on his front just next to the central reservation. It was very noticeable that the man was very still and was not wearing any shoes." Tobin, a Hell's Angel, was blasted by the gunman on the London-bound carriageway of the M40 near Leamington Spa. He was heading home after attending the Bulldog Bash at Long Marston Airport near Stratford – which was billed as Europe's biggest biker party. The Bulldog Bash organizer, a Hell's Angel who went by the name of Bilbo, said: "I knew the lad and you couldn't wish to meet a better person. We're used to deaths as bikers because people die in accidents. But, we don't expect someone to get shot. This is murder plain and simple and we have no idea why this has happened. We're just devastated. It is such a shame." It was unknown at the time whether Gerry had been targeted by a rival biker gang. The event itself had been massive, but had remained virtually trouble free. Police sealed off a large section of the M40 for hours after the murder at 2.30pm. A spokesman said: "The victim was travelling south towards London with a group of fellow bikers when he was shot in the head. It was a horrific incident, which we understand was witnessed by his friends. We are urging them to come forward so we can find out what happened. The victim was not pulled up on the hard shoulder, he was travelling at the time on a very busy motorway." The spokesman said detectives were investigating whether the killing was gang-related, and added that this would be one line of inquiry. An air ambulance rushed to the motorway but was unable to save the biker, who died from serious head injuries. The four-day Bulldog Bash had been attended by more than 30,000 bikers from all over the world. The festival, featuring music by Status Quo and The Wurzels, saw many bikers compete in head-to-head races that took place on a quarter-mile drag-strip. Stunt riders were also part of the event, as were an impressive array of custom bikes, jet cars and even jet lorries.

On 14th August 2007 it was reported that Tobin's murder was probably linked to a Hell's Angels feud. Gerry Tobin was executed as he travelled home from the festival. Police said they were investigating if a feud between rival chapters sparked the murder. His friends claimed that Tobin would have been more likely to be involved in stopping fights rather than starting them. Five Hell's Angels guarded the dead biker's flat in Mottingham, South London, close to the motorbike shop where he'd worked as an engineer. The M40 was reopened after forensic officers had spent more than 24 hours scoring the sealed-off area for clues. A postmortem confirmed that Tobin died from a single wound to the head. Grieving friends confirmed that Tobin's girlfriend, Rebecca Smith, was left devastated. Police tried to trace a green Rover 620 seen travelling close to Gerry, and also looked into a similar shooting after the festival six years before. In this attack, three bikers from Canada and France had been shot at from a car as they rode towards Oxford. Meanwhile, Rebecca Smith fought back tears as she branded Tobin's killer "callous and cowardly". She said: "Gerry stood out in a crowd as a true gentleman. He was a rare breed of man with the heart of a lion and a soul filled with compassion and selflessness. He was my soul mate and I feel blessed to have spent five years with such a wonderful man." Rebecca's statement was read out by Marcus Berriman, head of the Hell's Angels London chapter. Meanwhile, police confirmed they had received significant information about the killing.

In 2008, a chapter of Hell's Angels tried to murder Mick Jagger – but the plot capsized when their boat went down in a storm. The outrageous plan was revealed by a former FBI agent, who said the secret service infiltrated the biker gang. Some bikers pledged to kill Jagger at his New York seafront home after the Rolling Stones' 1968 Altamont concert. The band had hired Angels as security but, after one of them stabbed a fan to death, Jagger dumped them. Tom Mangold, who presented the Radio 4 series, *The FBI at 100*, said: "The Angels were so angered they decided to kill Jagger. A group of them took a boat to attack him from the sea to avoid security at the front. All were thrown overboard in a storm. They survived but there was not said to have been any further attempt on Jagger's life." A spokesman for Jagger said the plan sounded far-fetched.

More than a year after he was murdered, in November 2008, Tobin received justice when his killers were found guilty. Two members of the Outlaws were convicted of executing the rival Hell's Angel. A court heard how Tobin was ambushed as part of a long-running feud after leaving the Bulldog Bash. The Outlaws had been waiting for a "fully-patched" – meaning senior – Angel to stray on to their turf. They tailed the British-born man, who grew up in Canada, in a green Rover at up to 90mph, and pulled alongside him on the M40. Two gunmen fired from the car. One bullet struck Mr Tobin, while the other hit the bike's mudguard. Simon Turner, 41, from Nuneaton, and Dave Garside, 42, were both found guilty of murder and possessing a firearm with intent. A total of seven men – the entire South Warwickshire chapter of the Outlaws – were charged with the killing. A jury at Birmingham Crown Court then considered the verdicts on Malcolm Bull, 53, Karl Garside, 45, Dean Taylor, 47, and Ian Cameron, 46. Sean Creighton, 44, of Coventry, pleaded guilty before the trial and was to be sentenced later. Each of the seven men were found guilty, and the biker gang was jailed for life. Mr Justice Colman Treacy said the seven had callously shot dead a total stranger on the M40 simply because he was from a rival gang. He added: "Gerry Tobin was a totally innocent man. A decent man of good character. The utter pointlessness of what you did makes his murder more shocking. None of you have shown the slightest remorse." Turner and Taylor were jailed for a minimum of 30 years. Garside 27 years, his brother got 26 years, and Creighton got 28 years and six months. Bull and Cameron were each sentenced to a minimum of 25 years. Apart from Creighton, all members of the gang denied the charges. About 100 members of the Outlaws were at Birmingham Crown Court to see their fellow gang members sentenced.

At the beginning of 2013, Britain was bracing itself for a wave of deadly biker gang turf wars, which could have started rolling across Europe. Police warned that violent gangs from America, Canada and Australia – some armed with assault rifles and grenades – had arrived on the Continent. It raised fears that there would be a surge in violence as the "Outlaw Motorcycle

Gangs" (OMGs) battled it out for supremacy and control of organized crime markets. The UK had been put on alert by Europol, the EU's law enforcement agency, which said the arrival of the Comancheros and Rebels from Australia, Rock Machine from Canada, plus the Mongols and the Vagos from the USA had sparked tensions with established biker gangs.

The OMGs were said to be recruiting far-right militants, football hooligans and members from ex-military circles as they looked to gain control of drugs, gun and human-trafficking routes. But many of the gang members were not thought to be proper bikers – some did not even own a bike or have a driving licence.

The Outlaws have 30 chapters in England and Wales. Europol told British police to monitor UK gangs closely, and feared that a return of the Great Nordic Biker Wars of the 1990s – that left 12 dead and 100 others wounded – was imminent at the beginning of the New Year.

Large swathes of Denmark, Finland, Sweden and Norway saw rival gangs battle over "drug turfs". It began with a car park shoot-out that quickly escalated when an anti-tank rocket was fired at a Hell's Angels clubhouse. The war raged, with shootings, street assassinations and bombing. It ended after an innocent passer-by was killed by a car bomb. A Europol spokesman said: "Establishing a chapter on the turf of another gang is interpreted as an act of provocation. This is likely to result in violent confrontation which could include the use of rifles like Kalashnikovs and explosive devices such as grenades. Given the significant expansion of gangs in Europe, we have informed law enforcement partners of the risk of clashes."